ANGUS CULTURAL SERVICES

D1145059

S

**This book is to be returned on or before
the last date stamped below.**

LP.AKI

0 9 APR 2002

3 0 APR 2002

2 9 JUN 2002

MC 7/03
CC 11/03
SM 4/04

-7 JUN 2004

6 JUL 2004

2 3 NOV 2004

1 6 MAY 2005

1 0 JUN 2005

2 0 JUL 2005

2 4 MAR 2006

-3 JUL 2006

- 1 SEP 2006

28 OCT 2006

27 NOV 2006
NOV 08 I S
FEB 09 G T
JUN 09 A N
NOV 09 B T
APR 10 F P
JUL 10 A Z
OCT 10 M V
C S FEB 11
D O JUN 11
B Y SEP 11

M X MAR 12

A R JUN 12

I S APR 14

B R SEP 14

A Z MAR 15

B V SEP 15

F N FEB 15

F P JAN 17

- 6 SEP 2017

K Q SEP 17

ANGUSalive
Withdrawn from stock

Angus Council
CULTURAL SERVICES

U DEC 2001

SPECIAL MESSAGE TO READERS

This book is published under the auspices of

THE ULVERSCROFT FOUNDATION

(registered charity No. 264873 UK)

Established in 1972 to provide funds for research, diagnosis and treatment of eye diseases. Examples of contributions made are: —

A new Children's Assessment Unit at Moorfield's Hospital, London.

•

Twin operating theatres at the Western Ophthalmic Hospital, London.

•

A Chair of Ophthalmology at the University of Leicester.

•

The establishment of a Royal Australian College of Ophthalmologists "Fellowship".

You can help further the work of the Foundation by making a donation or leaving a legacy. Every contribution, no matter how small, is received with gratitude. Please write for details to:

THE ULVERSCROFT FOUNDATION,
The Green, Bradgate Road, Anstey,
Leicester LE7 7FU, England.
Telephone: (0116) 236 4325

In Australia write to:
THE ULVERSCROFT FOUNDATION,
c/o The Royal Australian College of
Ophthalmologists,
27, Commonwealth Street, Sydney,
N.S.W. 2010.

I've travelled the world twice over,
Met the famous: saints and sinners,
Poets and artists, kings and queens,
Old stars and hopeful beginners,
I've been where no-one's been before,
Learned secrets from writers and cooks
All with one library ticket
To the wonderful world of books.

© Janice James.

The wisdom of the ages
Is there for you and me,
The wisdom of the ages,
In your local library

There's large print books
And talking books,
For those who cannot see,
The wisdom of the ages,
It's fantastic, and it's free.

Written by Sam Wood, aged 92

FORTY YEARS ON
THE WILD FRONTIER

Noted Western historian Carl Breihan has culled from the handwritten diaries of John Montgomery, grandfather of co-author Wayne Montgomery, new facts about such legendary figures as Wyatt Earp, Doc Holliday and Bat Masterson and other famous and infamous men and women who gained notoriety when the Western Frontier was opened up. John Montgomery lived in the fabled town of Tombstone, Arizona, from 1870 to 1909, where he witnessed events of dramatic importance in the history of the American West.

CARL W. BREIHAN
AND
WAYNE MONTGOMERY

FORTY YEARS
ON THE
WILD FRONTIER

Complete and Unabridged

ULVERSCROFT
Leicester

First published in the
United States of America

First Large Print Edition
published 1997

Copyright © 1985 by
Carl W. Breihan and Wayne Montgomery
All rights reserved

British Library CIP Data

Breihan, Carl W. (Carl William), *1916 –*
Forty years on the wild frontier illustrated.
—Large print ed.—
1. Frontier and pioneer life—West (U.S.)
2. Large type books
I. Title II. Montgomery, Wayne
978'.02

ISBN 0–7089–3661–X

Published by
F. A. Thorpe (Publishing) Ltd.
Anstey, Leicestershire

Set by Words & Graphics Ltd.
Anstey, Leicestershire
Printed and bound in Great Britain by
T. J. Press (Padstow) Ltd., Padstow, Cornwall

This book is printed on acid-free paper

DEDICATED TO

ETHEL BREIHAN and
THYOLAIN MONTGOMERY,
OUR WIVES,
without whose constant encouragement
and understanding this book would
have never seen
the light of day.

Contents

Contents

Preface

Though many of the facts you are about to read may be familiar to you, this book presents them in a new way — directly from the journal of a man who lived a portion of them. Included, too, are other stories from the westward expansion of our nation that we learned of secondhand from those who lived those experiences. Then you will find those incidents that have been passed down by word of mouth, yet are so distinctly and authentically told that they cannot be dismissed as folktales. The characters in them live on in the memories of those who related them to us.

Truth, admittedly, is a many-faceted word. Definitions in dictionaries notwithstanding, in reality it is often that which a person wishes to believe.

During the course of our westward expansion the physical aspects of the Far West required a new breed of men. Many of these men reverted to an atavistic type that outsavaged the "savages" they despised. They disregarded, or rather ignored, the unfamiliar culture they encountered, as they could see no other than the one with which they were familiar. So two cultures clashed — one, in transition and with a more highly developed technology, moving in on a culture that evolved through centuries to meet the vagaries of the land it had long inhabited and called its own.

Some sections of this book show vividly the confrontations of these two cultures. Others are confrontations within the culture that slowly gained supremacy. Of the two, it is for the reader to decide which were the savages.

Most, if not all, of the persons appearing in the following pages were "little people," those who formed the backbone of the western expansion of this nation, who carried the politician's "Manifest Destiny" across the sere plains and the rugged mountains of our western lands to unite, mend, and soothe the anguish of a nation bloodied by a Civil War.

However the acquisition of our western lands required more bloodshed. This was supplied by the frontiersmen and the gunfighters and others of their breed. Some of the best-known among them — and also some of the least-known — figure in the following pages.

The murderer of John Ringo — thief, killer, drunk, and gunfighter — is named. This will cause controversy among Western historians. But John Montgomery's journal, the journals of his son, and the careful research of his grandson, Wayne Montgomery, provide firsthand, undeniable proof of incidents occurring in the Old West. Not least among them, of course, is the famous (and infamous) O.K. Corral Fight in Tombstone, Arizona.

Included in this thrilling account are the true stories concerning Frank Leslie, gunfighter of Tombstone, and Kate Bender the murderess of many lonely travelers on the Kansas prairie, among a host of others. And there is a brilliant account of the event American Labor will never forget, the Ludlow Massacre, in which Wayne Montgomery's father played a valiant role.

REX BUNDY, Historian
Victor, Montana

Introduction

JOHN MONTGOMERY operated a livery stable in Tombstone, Arizona, at the time of Wyatt Earp's highly publicized shootout there. Montgomery never wrote anything for publication, but he did record in a ledger every important event of his life. That ledger is preserved by his grandson, Wayne Montgomery, and much of this book has been taken from that handwritten account.

The material in Wayne's possession includes a good deal about the life of Coyote Smith, probably the West's most notorious killer whom John Montgomery knew well. In addition, Wayne's great-uncle, John Blane, left a written account of his capture by the Apache Indians and of his eventual escape with the aid of an old squaw.

★ ★ ★

1

John Montgomery was born in Menard County, Illinois, on July 17, 1830. When he was ten years old his father, Walter, and his mother, Mary, moved to the vicinity of Petersburg, Illinois, and settled on a farm located three miles from New Salem, where Abe Lincoln once ran a store with a partner named Barry, and for a time served as the village's first postmaster.

John grew up along the Sagamon River. There he became an expert marksman, supplying his family with game. Although he was not a man of violence, he spent most of his life hunting. He hated the farm, for wanderlust was in his blood, and he longed to go to the West to check the fascinating stories he had heard of its wonders. He married Elizabeth Bell, the daughter of a well-to-do farmer. After ten years of talking and planning they left Petersburg in the spring of 1861, and headed west in a covered wagon with their three children, a son named William and twin daughters, Cory and Cary.

They reached Fort Riley on May 20, 1861, two weeks ahead of other wagons that they knew would be in their train

2

under the direction of John Young, a professional in this business of leading contingents toward the West. Everyone joining this project had to pay a certain fare and had to own a good team and wagon, one extra horse, a spare wheel, and money and food enough to last to the end of the journey.

Many such parties never arrived at their destination, especially if they were farmers from the East, who knew nothing of the conditions they would have to meet — such travelers were "sitting ducks" for the Indians. Thousands of unmarked graves lie along the Santa Fe Trail and other routes. Many whole trains disappeared from the face of the earth and were never heard from again. Those organized by John Young, however, got through, for he was experienced in dealing with the Indians and finding grass and water. Furthermore, he understood windstorms and how great herds of buffalo roamed the plains. For this reason John Montgomery and his family had chosen to go along in the party he led.

Before their departure on the first of June 1861, Captain Young spent two hours explaining the difficulties ahead. He made it plain that he was in command and that his orders would have to be obeyed if they wanted to reach their destination. He assured them that any member could leave the train at any time he should desire.

Through the heat and dust Young rode in front with six wagons loaded with hard-to-get supplies that he planned to sell in Denver. One scout rode in the rear one on each side, and one along the column on the watch.

For a while nothing of great importance occurred. There were thirty-six wagons in all, quite a train when strung out. Each wagon had its own place in line, where it would remain unless Young directed otherwise. No shots were to be fired at anything other than by Young's orders. A howl went up when he ordered the members to get rid of their dogs. They claimed that dogs would let them know when Indians were about. Young pointed out that the dogs would also let the Indians know where they camped. The dogs were disposed of in one way or another.

In John Montgomery's record only the highlights of the crossing are noted. The train was accosted once by Yellow Dog, an Osage Chief, who demanded whiskey and guns, but got only food, cloth for the Indian women, and some flour which the squaws liked to spread on their faces on festive occasions. The days were so hot and unbearable that the women in the train often let down their hair and went barefoot, something considered sinful back home.

All the way out they kept near the Smoky Hill River. It was a godsend, for it gave the travelers a chance to bathe in the cool waters. All fires were extinguished at night, and there was never any loud talking or singing. These people were so trail-weary when supper was over that they fell into their blankets and slept until they were awakened.

Before they had been on the trail many days everybody began to realize what they were in for. Some cursed the day they had left home. Others grumbled at everything, mostly at the vast plains. Nothing could be seen for miles in any direction, and the only trees were along the river. For days on end they never encountered a human being except those in the train.

John Montgomery wrote: "I wonder how a man like Young can make this crossing time and time again, always seeming as fresh every day as when he started."

Once they heard a buffalo stampede, thunder on a clear day. Captain Young knew how dangerous such a thing could be.

"I've seen towns wiped out, wagon trains destroyed, because the buffalo stop for nothing. They run madly in every direction," he told them.

He led the train into the only place where they might be comparatively safe — a grove of cottonwood trees — and they waited for hours. Luckily, the stampede missed them by raging off westward.

Twice they were struck by windstorms. The first did not do much damage, since Young led the train behind a high hill until it passed. The next one caught them in the open. It upset wagons, tore off canvas tops, and by the time it was over considerable damage had been caused. Many of the wagons arrived at Fort Wallace with no canvas cover at all. No one was seriously injured, however.

Another time a scout rode in to report a heavy dust cloud to the north, coming on fast. The wagons huddled in a circle. They were surrounded by about fifty hostile young braves. Before any damage was done a detachment of cavalry rode in, and the Indians fled. The cavalry gave chase, and again the train escaped unharmed.

The trip so far as Pond Creek Station (later named Fort Wallace) took almost two months, primarily because of the great herds of buffalo, which twice halted the train for two days. At that point almost all the members were ready to give up. Many of them remained in the area, where there was plenty of water. The surrounding country was ideal for raising cattle, and the fort protected them to a degree.

Not so John Montgomery. When Captain Young set out for Denver he and his family were with him. By the time they reached that mile-high settlement cold weather had set in.

He remained in that area for several years, partly skinning a six-line team for a freight company and partly hunting buffalo, which brought him a fine profit. Here he first met Coyote Smith, a character feared by all frontiersmen and even by the Indians. During the two years they prospected together Smith told him the story of his life, which John Montgomery wrote down in his ledger.

John's first wife died in 1869. He took his children to Wier City, Kansas, to live with relatives. In 1870 he remarried and moved with his children to Tombstone, Arizona.

There he was to witness events of dramatic importance in the history of the West.

Our John Montgomery is not to be confused with another of the same name, who also lived in Tombstone and happened to own the O.K. Corral, together with a man named Benson. This John Montgomery served for a time as supervisor of Cochise County. He died in 1909 and is buried in Tombstone. He never married.

Coyote Smith

AS with many another frontiersman, little has been written about Coyote Smith. Historians of that period recorded what they considered historically significant and bypassed events and individuals whose importance they did not then recognize. Numerous men and woman, had their experiences been recorded, would now be remembered as well as Buffalo Bill, Billy the Kid, and others. John Montgomery left his account of all that Coyote Smith related to him, as well as of incidents he learned about from Smith's daughter (who lived until 1964) and from the Colorado Historical Society.

Scott Andrew Smith was his name. He was born on April 15, 1842, a short distance east of St. Joseph, Missouri. He reached manhood sound of body and mind despite his being a freak of nature in one respect — he was a veritable beanpole. At eighteen years of age he stood six feet four inches tall and weighed a hundred and fifty pounds. Yet he had the agility of a deer and the prowess of a mountain lion.

His formal education was limited, partly because during his school days his ungainly physique made him a prime object of ridicule. Many a boy who made fun of him returned home with a swollen eye and a puffed lip. One day, after Smith struck a boy who taunted him, the boy's father attacked Smith with a bullwhip. Determining on revenge, Smith stealthily followed the man for days. One night, when the man was weaving his way home in a drunken stupor Smith waylaid him with a club, then stabbed him to death with a knife.

Smith was, of course, suspected, but by the time the authorities arrived he had headed west with a wagon train and was nowhere to be found. Some of the men he met along the way made fun of him, at least until they learned to leave him alone after several of them were kicked into unconsciousness by Smith's flying feet. He never used his fists. When an enemy got close enough, he jumped feet first and struck like the kick of a horse.

By the age of twenty-one Smith was well known to whites along the trails as a man possessed of the devil, and Indians called him "brother of the evil spirit." It was rumored that he ate human flesh and killed men just for the fun of seeing them fall.

In speaking of this to Montgomery, Smith branded it a lie, but he admitted, "All Indians need killing, and I never killed even a white man who didn't need killing." He added, "One day after I had helped bury a family — a father mother and ten children killed by Indians — I vowed to kill every Indian that crossed my path."

His first Indian was a young boy who was dragging a white baby behind his horse. Smith ran down this Indian, killed him, cut him wide open with his knife, and buried the child.

The name 'Coyote' came from Smith's habit of killing every coyote he saw, and he was a crack shot from a moving wagon. Whenever the other men tied his wrists to keep him from shooting recklessly, he bulged his wrist muscles.

When he relaxed them, the rope or whatever he was tied with came loose. He carried a razor-sharp knife at the back of his neck, out of sight and tied down. With a jerk he could throw this with the accuracy and speed of a striking snake. This saved his life many times.

In 1867 the *Leavenworth Times* reported that he was engaged to scout a train through to Fort Wallace. It consisted of fifty wagons loaded with barrels of whiskey. Headed by a wagonmaster named Captain Bill Martin, the train was accompanied by a cavalry lieutenant, six private soldiers, four scouts, and three wranglers. These, along with a driver for each wagon, made quite a company, each man armed with a single-shot carbine, breech loader and carrying a .45 calibre muzzle-loading revolver and several extra loaded cylinders. If need be, these could be reloaded quickly.

Smith carried the only repeating rifle on the train, a 16–shot Winchester rimfire, .44 calibre, designed by Tyler Henry. He wasn't satisfied at all with the way things were organized, especially when he saw Indians helping to load the whiskey and other supplies. It was all too likely that they would send word ahead to their friends and relatives of the cargo being transported, and the train would be intercepted. But he was being paid fifty dollars for the trip, considerable money in those hectic days, so he went along.

The wagons left Fort Riley about the middle of May 1867. A week out, Smith was scouting behind the train when three Indians tried to ride him down. He killed one of them, and the others fled. Later a chief caught up with them under a truce flag and demanded that Smith be punished for killing a friendly Indian. Smith called the chief a few vile names and told the cavalry lieutenant his version of what had happened. When the chief persisted that Smith should fight one of his braves to the death barehanded, the daring young man was pleased to accept the challenge.

The brave selected was much heavier than Smith, and Captain Martin tried to intervene and call the whole thing off. Smith was undaunted.

"The Indian never lived that I can't whip," he told Martin.

They squared off, and the buck immediately rushed Smith, obviously intending to grab and tear him in two. Instead, he found himself on his back, for Smith had kicked him in the chest with both his feet. Again the Indian tried rushing, and again he found himself looking up at the blue sky. When he saw he was losing, he gestured to the chief for help. The chief threw him a knife, despite the agreed-upon rules. The buck stood facing Smith, ready to cut him down. He swiped at Smith, but the knife struck only empty air. Then Smith jerked his knife from the back of his neck and threw it into the buck's belly up to the hilt. In a few minutes the buck expired. The chief threatened Captain Martin that he would return and capture the whole train.

When they had traveled to within about a hundred miles of their destination, Smith warned Martin, "Things are going too well. Don't let your guard down. We won't be safe until we get inside Fort Wallace."

Martin laughed this off and reminded Smith, "I've got enough men to stand off any kind of a raid."

Later when Smith was scouting five miles to the rear of the train, he noticed a dust cloud on the horizon. He knew it was either a company of soldiers or Indians. He soon discovered that it was a band of Cheyennes wearing war paint.

He reported to Martin, "A band of about a hundred and fifty are riding hard upon us."

The train was circled and the stock placed inside. Each wagon was supplied with thick boards to lay against the wheels for protection against the attack, for this had saved many lives in the past.

The braves rode in close, screaming and yelling. Some were armed with rifles, some with bows and arrows, some with only lances and knives. At the first contact several were unhorsed, and one fell wounded near Smith's position. Smith pulled him inside the circle and tried in vain to get him to reveal how many Indians were in the party.

When he refused to speak, Smith killed him. The other men in the train didn't like this, but Smith wasn't interested in whether they approved or not; he had rid the West of one more Indian.

After the first rush the Indians made several more light attacks and then rode off.

Martin said, "They won't attack at night, and we'll be ready for them in the morning."

Coyote Smith told him, "The only reason they don't usually attack at night is that they like to see what they are fighting, but it doesn't mean they won't come back after dark this time. I've seen them attack at night several times."

That night was so black that a man couldn't see his hand in front of him, and things became alarmingly quiet. About midnight the Indians struck — four hundred of them, all screeching. Though the men of the train fought bravely, it was useless. In an hour's time only four men on the train were still alive: the cavalry lieutenant, Coyote Smith, a scout named Ramsey, and Captain Bill Martin.

Smith crawled into a ravine, lay on his back, and covered himself with leaves and brush. He was extremely thin, and didn't need much room to hide. There he remained, with an arrow through his shoulder and a bullet in his hip. When daylight arrived he slowly raised his head and looked around. Seeing no Indians, he staggered to his feet and was shocked at the sight before him. The wagons had been looted, pushed together and set afire after the bodies of all the dead men had been piled on top of them. Since they were in a deep buffalo wallow, the flames did not set the dry grass afire, so they were only slightly burned.

He searched for a gun without success. However he still had his knife. He headed for the Smoky Hill River careful not to expose himself. He removed the arrow from his shoulder; the bullet in his hip would have to wait. On the river bank he bathed the wounds and searched for some mold to put on them, an old Indian practice. An ordinary man would have died, but Smith was a man of almost superhuman stamina. He rested all day in the underbrush, listening to the Indians celebrating on the whiskey they had stolen from the train.

At dusk he crawled to a small rise and surveyed the area. Hundreds of drunken Indians were lying on the ground in a

17

stupor. Fifty gallon whiskey barrels, now empty, stood about. He spotted the place where the horses were tied and devised a plan that might help even the score.

After dark he crawled to the horses, got a rope on one, and drew it back from the corral. He cut hair from several horses' tails and made a torch, which he fastened to a long stick. The surrounding grass was about two feet high and completely dry. When he set it afire near the horses, they broke loose and ran. He then circled the camp, setting fire to the grass as he went. There was a brisk wind from the south, and in minutes a roaring prairie fire had begun. He rode to a hill and watched.

He later said; "Never in my life had I seen such confusion. The fire burnt right over the sleeping Indians, while they jumped screaming and ran for the horses, only to find them gone."

Smith then mounted the single horse he had caught and rode to a homestead the train had passed the previous day, where a man, woman, and two children had been living. He found the man and woman butchered; the two children were nowhere to be seen. He figured at first that the children had been taken captive. Nevertheless, he called and called. He was on the point of leaving when he heard them yelling. He found them in a weed patch near the creek, frightened almost to death.

He took the children to a nearby town — perhaps it was Russell, though this is not certain. From there he sent a message to the army, reporting the massacre. The children were taken in by a family, and Smith was treated by a doctor. Soon he was back on the prairie hunting Indians. Many of them would pay with their lives for the massacre.

Later that same year 1867, the *Leavenworth Times* carried a news item dated from Western Union Line, Junction City, Kansas:

A man came into Salina about fifty miles west of here, on Friday, and reported a frightful massacre of white men by Cheyennes, near the head of the Smoky Hill route a few days ago. As Wallace's train with sixty-three men were camped, a party of several hundred Indians surrounded them and murdered fifty-nine of the sixty-three whites.

One of the four who escaped had an arrow wound in his shoulder and a bullet wound in his hip.

A year later on his way to Denver Smith stopped at a creek to water his two horses and two dogs.

"The dogs were my scouts," he said, "for they can smell an Indian a mile away, and they hate them as much as I do."

Just as he started to leave he noticed the hounds bristle. He knew the sign — Indians were close by.

He led his horses back off the trail and skinned up a tall pine. From there he saw what he was looking for; three bucks squatted before a fire. He descended, grabbed his rifle, circled until he had the wind in the right direction. He wanted to take them by surprise. Noiselessly he jumped into their midst. All three leaped to their feet. He pumped a few rounds into them. One fell dead. Another though wounded, began backing off slowly with the third. Smith killed him before he got far. Whereupon the other broke and ran as fast as he could. He didn't make it. Smith brought him down with a shot in the back. After dragging all three bodies off the trail, he took their scalps and hung them from a tree where they could be found by other Indians. He then mutilated the bodies and with his animals continued on his journey to Denver.

Some men on hearing this tale, believed Smith exaggerated. Those who knew him better swore by what he said.

In Denver Smith left his horses and dogs in a livery stable, knowing that the dogs would not leave the horses unless he himself called them. He paid the stableman and started to leave, after placing his pistol and rifle in the pack he carried. He headed for a hotel, where he planned to clean up and go on a spree. It had been a long time since he had given himself a celebration.

As he crossed the wagonyard, he was stopped by three tough-looking customers. One of them poked a gun into his belly.

"Smith," said the man with the gun, "I am going to kill you, you no-good bastard. You'll never kill another man with a knife like you did my brother."

Smith answered in a soft, low voice, because he was in a bad spot and knew it.

"Mister if you kill an unarmed man in this town you'll hang, sure as hell."

The man thought for a second or two, then replied, "Hold right where you are, and I'll get you a gun."

The man turned his head to speak to his friends. Smith, swift as a snake, drew his knife from behind his neck and threw it deep into the man's chest. His two friends started toward Smith, but were stopped by John Montgomery, a pedestrian who happened by in time to witness the affair. When the two strangers saw the cocked carbine Montgomery pointed in their direction, they backed off.

This gave Smith a chance to draw his pistol from his pack. He didn't get a chance to use it, for the sheriff took him in hand. The man Smith killed was evidently not Denver's favorite son, and the sheriff soon turned Smith loose after several local men had spoken in his behalf.

Smith thanked John Montgomery for his timely assistance and said, "After I clean up I'll meet you for a drink."

When Smith arrived later in a saloon, his ungainly figure, in a black suit and bow tie, reminded Montgomery of what an undertaker usually looked like. They had a few drinks and talked of the West, then entered into a poker game that lasted all night. Smith was a heavy winner. Still, Montgomery broke about even.

Smith was the center of attraction among men who knew him or had heard about him. John Montgomery was warned to keep clear of Smith or he would be found dead in some alley. Contrary to this prediction, the two became fast friends. Before the week was out they planned a prospecting trip.

Prior to leaving Smith bet a man that he could outrun his horse in two hundred yards. He told John to bet all he had on him, that the horse never lived he couldn't outrun in that distance. John bet on Smith — and won. John said that when the gun cracked for the start Smith was already hallway to the finish, before the horse even got started.

The next day they replenished their shrunken supplies and headed south for Colorado Springs, an area they had heard about. About fifty miles south of Denver they turned due west. When they had almost reached the mountains, the dogs let them know Indians were in the vicinity. They discovered they were being followed by six Indians. They led their horses back off the trail and holed up among rocks to await the attack.

When the trailing Indians were about two hundred yards away Smith knocked one down with a .45 –.70 buff (buffalo) gun, and the others immediately hit the ground. Smith didn't want this; he wanted them to charge so that he could use his repeating Winchester.

Turning to John, he said, "Take the animals and head west, and I'll overtake you later."

Two hours later Smith caught up to him with an arrow through his side. "But we won't fool with it now," he cautioned. "We'll move out. Those devils might return with help, for I killed two of them."

At dark they made camp off the trail near a creek. Smith took a couple of stiff drinks and instructed John how to remove the arrow.

"Cut off the arrowhead, stand on my arm, and when I tell you, jerk out the shaft."

John did as instructed. As the blood flew, Smith only grunted. Then he gave John further instructions as to the dressing of the wound.

"Look along the creek for mold on a rotted log. Place it on either side of the arm, place a piece of bark on each wound, and tie it securely with a buckskin bond."

This done, they settled back for the night. John spent most of the time awake, fearful that the Indians might sneak up on them. Now and then Smith would take a drink of whiskey.

A few days later John removed the poultice from his friend's side. The bleeding had stopped. The wound looked terrible, but gave no sign of infection. A fresh poultice was applied. Smith must have suffered considerably for two weeks; after that he began to mend rapidly. A month later they packed up and resumed their journey.

About this time John Montgomery began to copy down Smith's stories in his ledger. This pleased Smith, and he readily gave out all the information he could.

He said he had been captured several times, once by an old squaw and her man. On this particular occasion he had gone to sleep under a bush after prowling the Kansas prairie for game (Indians) without finding anything worthwhile. From high up in a tall cottonwood tree he saw nothing for miles around except buffalo. Leaving his animals some distance off, he decided to get a few winks while he could.

He was awakened by a knife at his throat, held by an Indian squaw. He knew better than to move violently, so he barely breathed as he waited. Her husband tied his hands and feet. This done, they shook out his pack and ate his food, sharing it with a little boy of about six years of age. They laughed at Smith's predicament, and the boy threw rocks at him, being very deft at this art. They talked of how the great chief would reward them when they presented him with the Evil One alive. Evidently they knew Smith by reputation.

When they were ready to leave, the buck came near to cut loose Smith's feet so that he could straddle a horse. At that instant Smith threw his knife from the back of his neck deep into the buck's body. Had they been aware of Smith's ability to loosen his hands by relaxing his muscles, they would have killed him while they had the chance. Before Smith could retrieve his knife from the mortally wounded buck, the squaw grabbed his rifle and tried desperately to fire it. Failing to make it work, she grabbed the barrel and began swinging it at Smith. She was as strong as a brave, and he had difficulty keeping out of her reach.

When she failed to hit him, she again tried to fire at him. This gave him a chance to regain his knife. He cut himself loose and jumped to his feet. As soon as the squaw saw that he had the knife, she dropped the rifle and pulled her little boy close to her. Evidently she felt her time had come, and stood bravely waiting for him to throw the knife at her. Her bravery got to Smith. He wanted to kill her but just couldn't do it.

He had seen Indian men wilt under similar circumstances.

He told her "Take the boy and go."

She asked for a horse, which he refused. She headed out across the prairie, dragging the bewildered child behind her.

In another of his experiences with Indians Smith described how he was led into a trap by Osages after he had killed and mutilated three of their men. He had spotted three bucks riding in front of him. They had evidently not yet seen him. If they had, they'd have put up a fight. He wanted all three of those bucks. When he got close to them, they broke into a full gallop as though to outdistance him. The next thing he knew he was surrounded by a hundred warriors. The only thing that saved him was their chief's standing order to bring him in alive.

They took his rifle and pistol, but failed to find the knife he always kept behind his head against his back. After tying him hand and foot, they threw him across the back of a horse, and set out for their Osage village.

He said in relating this: "I was hard put to keep from losing my knife, but I held my head back as far as possible to keep the knife in its sheath. I knew that without this weapon I didn't have a chance."

In the center of the village he was tied to a pole for all to see. The children threw rocks at him while the squaws poked him unmercifully with sharp sticks. When darkness set in, he was hauled before the chief, whose name was Three Horses.

The chief taunted Smith, "You are not the brother of the evil spirit. You are the brother of a jack rabbit."

He ordered his men to disrobe the captive. When they cut him loose from the pole, he jumped forward and threw his knife into the midsection of the chief. In the confusion Smith was forgotten, as everybody ran to aid the fallen chief.

Quick as a flash Smith was out

of the camp, running like a deer northward. Later he turned west, then south. He ran all night and at dawn came to a homestead, where he hid behind the barn and called to those inside. A man came out carrying a shotgun, demanding, "What's going on here?" Smith explained his situation and said he wanted to borrow a horse and a pair of pants. Later Smith returned the horse and paid the homesteader in gold for his hospitality.

Smith said he knew the Indians couldn't follow him in the darkness, and, believing he couldn't get far on foot, they would expect soon to overtake him in daylight. Sometime later he learned that the chief had not died from the knife thrust, so he hung around to watch the tribe.

One day he saw the chief lead out several braves. He got ahead of them and waited for their approach. He was about two hundred yards away. It would have been difficult to shoot at a moving target at that distance. Still, he had to try. He rested his .47 –.70 over a tree limb, took careful aim, and pulled the trigger.

The chief fell from his horse dead. By the time his followers decided to set out after the assailant, Smith was some distance away.

Perhaps it was in 1870 — the exact date is uncertain — when Smith was engaged to scout a train from Fort Riley to Santa Fe, in New Mexico Territory. Everything progressed in good order until they were well into New Mexico, where they were attacked several times by a band of Apaches. They managed to ward off the attack until a large band struck them from all sides and split the train. Their losses were heavy, and two women and two children were taken captive.

Smith pulled into an army post (probably Fort Union) to ask for help in getting the captives back alive. The commanding officer immediately dispatched a runner to try to make a trade of some sort, but the runner failed to return.

Many Indian scouts worked both sides, selling information to the army and also to the Indians. Smith refused to take the wagon train on from the fort until the captives were returned. He became disgusted by the delay, as nothing was being done to ransom the whites, and decided to act on his own.

He had discovered, by asking questions, that the chief of this band of raiders had twin daughters about six years old. Twins were not common among Indians, especially girl twins. In many cases girl twins were both killed at birth, and if the twins were boys it was usual to have one killed. But this chief, Black Bull, for some incomprehensible reason was very proud of these two girls and kept them under close supervision continually.

By observing the camp closely for some time, Smith devised a plan he thought might work. He would have to locate a renegade trader and get him to deliver several gallons of whiskey to this camp and present it to the chief. He never knew of an Indian to refuse whiskey, especially if it was free.

He found a trader who agreed to deliver the whiskey when he saw Smith's money. Smith told the trader "If the whiskey's not delivered, I'll send them your head on a pole."

Smith returned to his vantage point to watch results. In good time the trader delivered the whiskey to the chief as a present. The chief no doubt figured that the trader was after something, but whatever it was could wait. He called in his braves and a few squaws to help in celebrating. They hogged the whiskey as usual. Soon they became drunk, many staggering off to their respective tepees to sleep it off. The chief outlasted them all, but finally retired.

Smith slithered noiselessly toward the chief's tepee. He slit a hole in the skin cover and entered like a blind person feeling his way about. He found the chief dead asleep. Next he found the little girls. When he

34

touched the squaw she gasped and sat upright, so he laid her low with his gun butt. He grabbed one child and placed his hand over her mouth so that she couldn't cry out, then he made his way with her to where he had tied his horse and headed for the fort. He rode as fast as was safe — fast riding at night on the desert could be dangerous because of the terrain, and he didn't want to hurt the child. He also knew that every Indian in that area would shortly be on his trail.

Smith reported to the commanding officer what he had done and asked him to send a scout to the chief to arrange a trade. A scout was dispatched with instructions to tell the chief that the army had his child. In a few hours the white captives were returned unharmed, and the trade was made. Later, the cavalry raided this camp and killed twenty-five Indians.

Often when whites were taken captive and held for ransom, if the ransom was not paid as quickly as expected, the whites were killed, or else a raid was made on the village and the whites were then killed.

Perhaps these stories seem a little farfetched, but there were scouts capable of extraordinary accomplishments. One was Amos Chapman. If his bravery at a buffalo fight should be shown in a movie, the audience would consider it impossible. Actually, he carried a wounded soldier several hundred feet while under fire by twenty Indians. He had one of his feet shot off, yet he did not drop the soldier he was carrying. He made it back to camp. For this deed he was granted the Congressional Medal of Honor. Amos Chapman was the only civilian ever to receive this award. Yet until recently he was bypassed by historians.

General Custer was known to say: "Most army scouts are worthless, for all they want is a place to eat and sleep. But now and then one comes along like Smith or Chapman who never finds an assignment too difficult."

It is true that Coyote Smith, by redeeming the captives from Chief Black Bull, won the goodwill of the people of the wagon train, and his reward was the feeling that comes to a man when he has done something worthwhile. After he had delivered the train safely at Santa Fe, he returned to the Kansas plains, where he felt more at home.

"In Kansas," he said, "we don't have to meet with Apache cunning. An Apache can almost track a bird in flight."

He had not been in Kansas long when he picked up the trail of three Indians. He followed them at a safe distance, not wanting to be led into another trap. He soon discovered that they were not native to the Kansas area, but were from a tribe in Oklahoma. He knew they were on the prowl when he saw them ride up and survey a lone homestead. He circled them to give warning to the occupants. The Indians saw him and charged to cut him off. He continued toward the house, yelling, "Indians!" When he reached it, he jumped from his horse and roughly shoved the lady inside and slammed the door behind them both, just as his three pursuers rode up.

Smith opened a window and saw a man come staggering across the field with an arrow in his back. Again the Indians rode by, and Smith toppled one from his horse. The others retreated into the prairie. He helped the field man into the house and removed the arrow from where it had struck the fleshy part of his side. He then gathered mold from the springhouse and dressed the wound. This done, the man was loaded into a spring wagon, and he headed for a neighbor's house three miles away.

The lady kept telling Smith, "Around here Indians is friendly. They wouldn't hurt us — we know 'em. You riled 'em up."

But Smith explained, "All Indians look alike to some people, but these

Indians were out to raid and kill. They were from Oklahoma, not native to Kansas."

Smith left his animals and set out afoot, looking for the two Indians who had escaped. About dark he found them camped on the bank of the Arkansas River. He crawled slowly through the underbrush until he was almost upon them and then jumped into the open.

At sight of him they went into action. He hadn't scared them. When he threw his knife at one, the other grabbed him, causing him to lose his rifle. It became a desperate hand-to-hand battle. Eventually Smith got his thumbs into the buck's throat and choked him to death. This bit of action taught him not to take too much for granted.

While Montgomery and Smith were mining gold, as they neared their base camp one night they were held up by two men who cocked rifles at their heads. The strangers demanded gold. Smith handed some over to them, saying, "That's all we have."

The day had been especially lucrative for Montgomery and Smith, so the outlaws were in luck, but they failed to find the gold hidden in the camp. They tied Smith and Montgomery hand and foot, took their fine Winchesters, their horses, and whatever else suited their fancy, and left.

Smith soon had his hands and feet untied by his method of relaxing his muscles, then released Montgomery.

"Mind camp and wait for me," he told his friend, "because I'll be back even if it takes a few days. I'm gonna run those two worthless skunks down, and I'll get back all they took from us."

At a nearby camp he borrowed a rifle for himself and asked one of the neighbors to take another over to John. They offered him a horse, such as it was, which he declined, knowing he would be better off on foot.

Three days after the holdup Smith

returned with the horses and other things that had been taken, and all he said was, "I rid the world of two more worthless pieces of humanity?"

A miner several months later told Montgomery what had happened, and his version concurred with Smith's own story.

The way the miner told it, two mounted men rode into a certain camp one evening and asked for food. While they were busy eating, the tallest man he ever saw walked in, carrying a rifle. He pointed the rifle at the two men, disarmed them, and told the miners in the camp what these two had done to him and John.

He said to the miners, "I'm going to give these two varmints a chance to fight for their worthless lives, a damn sight more 'n they gave John and me."

He jerked one of the outlaws to the road and threw him a revolver, which landed at the man's feet. The man reached quickly for the gun,

41

and, as he straightened up, Smith threw a knife into his heart.

Smith then ordered the other man, "Come out and fight," but the man refused to move. Smith obtained a rope, placed it around the man's neck, and dragged him to a tree. After he died, Smith picked up both bodies and threw them into a deep ravine.

Smith gathered his and John's belongings from the dead men's packs, recovered their two horses, rifles, and whatever else he could find, and departed, leaving behind a bunch of dumbfounded miners.

Smith and Montgomery worked the streams in what was later one of the biggest strikes in the West — Cripple Creek to Central City. They didn't make a big strike, though they did very well. Afterward they both headed back to Denver, where, still friends, they dissolved their partnership.

In the fall of 1880, Montgomery, crossing Allen Street in Tombstone where he had moved, looked to the west and saw a man leading a horse behind the one he was riding, followed by two hound dogs. Closer observation identified Coyote Smith. He rode up, dismounted, and greeted Montgomery as though they had parted company only the day before.

After a few drinks in a nearby saloon, Smith said he had come to Tombstone because he had heard money was to be made there. Montgomery invited him to stay at his home until he found a place to live.

Smith replied, "John, you know damn well I can't sleep indoors. I have to live in the open, so I'll see you later."

For a while Montgomery saw Smith now and then. One day Smith told him, of all things, that he had met and married a Mexican woman who lived on a small place she owned, and he asked Montgomery to pay them a visit.

Coyote Smith had moved inside! No one at Tombstone knew him

by reputation, and Montgomery let it go at that, telling nobody about Smith's past.

He didn't see much of Smith until the spring of 1881, when Smith was jailed for murder. Montgomery called on him at the jail, and Smith said he had killed a man who was fooling around his wife. He claimed he killed the man with a knife in self-defense. Nothing could be done. Smith would have to remain in jail for trial.

Some time later when Montgomery visited him in jail, Smith told him a surprising story. A lawyer or a man who represented himself as a lawyer told Smith that if he could come up with a thousand dollars, he would arrange for him to escape; otherwise they would hang him, sure as hell, for he didn't have a chance, regardless of his self-defense story. Smith made the arrangements and gave this character the thousand dollars. He did not see the man again, not in Tombstone at any rate. He should have seen through such a proposition, of course.

Smith was tried and acquitted. After some investigation Montgomery found out for Smith that the man who had swindled him was actually a lawyer named Larson, who had, by all accounts, come from Kansas City. Smith bade Montgomery farewell. They never met again.

The rest of this story came from Smith's granddaughter in St. Joseph, Missouri.

Smith made his way to Kansas City, and found the man's address. When he came around and knocked on the door, the man almost fainted. Smith told him, "I want my money, or I'll kill you."

Larson pleaded that he didn't have that much money.

"Get it," Smith ordered.

Larson said, "Then I'll have to steal it."

Smith answered, "I don't give a damn where you get it. Just get it."

One night Larson had Smith accompany him to a saloon after closing hours, saying he knew where the owner hid his money. Smith waited outside to be paid, and he was paid. Whether all the money came from the saloon is not known, but Smith got it. After that he took off for the West, parts unknown. The next day Larson was arrested, for Smith had left behind a note for the police. What he got out of this, if anything, we don't know. I guess Smith figured the score was even.

The next heard of Smith was that he had been arrested for killing an army sergeant. After a term in the Kansas State Prison he returned to St. Joseph, where he died in 1915.

There was another man in Tombstone who called himself Coyote Smith, but he was only a law abiding millworker not to be confused with the Smith of this story.

Following a Dream to the West

Back in Petersburg, Illinois, John Montgomery's nephew, John Blane, kept a diary that was discovered by me as late as 1946. This story is taken from it. — W.M.

BY arrangement, my friend Ellis Williams met me on April first, 1867, because since we were small children we had talked about going West. Had we any idea of what was in store for us we'd have stayed at home. But we were now eighteen years old and had reached full maturity. Ellis was a bigger man than I was in stature — about six feet tall and weighing two hundred pounds. I was five feet ten and weighed a hundred and eighty. Prior to this meeting we have been hampered by lack of funds, but now Ellis's grandfather had passed away, leaving him considerable money and land.

47

This day the first thing he said when we met was, "John, are you ready to go?"

"Go where?" I asked.

And he replied, "Out West. I'll lend you the money, and you can repay me later when we strike it rich?"

We were both rich then, had we brains enough to realize it.

I told him, "I'm ready when you are."

So, against the advice of all our relatives, we began making preparations for the trip. We bought two of the finest riding horses money could buy — both were big, high-strung, and could run like deer. We decided we'd buy supplies in St. Louis. We had heard of the Henry Winchesters that fired sixteen rounds, and breech-loading revolvers — these also we would buy in St. Louis.

On April tenth we set out for St. Louis, about as happy as two young boys can be. We were on our way at last and had everything we needed — except experience. We were both expert rifle and pistol shots, from hunting and much practice.

We found St. Louis a beehive of activity. It seemed as though every person in the East was heading west in search of free land. We bought Winchesters, pistols, ammunition, and whatever supplies we would need until we reached Kansas City, Missouri.

At Boonville we almost met our undoing. Ellis and I went into a saloon for a few drinks, and Ellis got into a poker game, which ended in a fight when Ellis accused a gambler of cheating. The man jumped to his feet, and Ellis knocked him down. He came up with a gun in his hand, and Ellis killed him. He was not arrested, but we were ordered to leave town at once.

We vowed to each other to keep out of trouble from now on. We reached Kansas City without mishap. We did not spend much time there. The place was covered with the scum of the earth, and a man had to keep a close eye on his belongings. News of the killing had preceded us, and we were left pretty well alone. We were advised by a lawman to move on, because the man Ellis had killed had many friends along the river. We set out for Fort Riley without delay.

An old Indian scout warned us not to let an Indian come close under a flag of truce.

"When they get close enough," he said, "kill a couple, and they'll likely leave you alone. If it's a big party, just outrun them. A small band you can't see too far off, but a big band you can by the dust."

With this in mind we headed for Denver and the gold fields. We met many folks returning who advised us to return home, but we didn't consider such a thing. About five days beyond Fort Riley we discovered that we were being followed by eight Indians. We rode into a gulley and prepared to fight. We could have ridden on, but we wanted to show them how competent we were. They split and rode on each side of us. We pumped more lead at them in a few seconds than they had dreamed of.

The next time they all came in from the front. This charge was made, I believe, to make us do something crazy. Then they veered off, except one, and he

50

charged right into our position, jumped from his horse, and grabbed Ellis. I figured Ellis could handle him, so I kept pumping lead at the others, but they went out of range. When I turned to Ellis and the struggling brave, Ellis had choked him almost to death. I pulled him off, and the brave fell out cold.

When he recovered his breathing, we gave him a drink of whiskey and made ready to leave. The others didn't make any effort to charge again. We mounted and got out of there in a hurry. We had made another mistake and vowed to be more careful after that.

The Great Plains were so continuous that we came to the conclusion we must be riding in a circle, though the compass indicated we were still heading west.

About halfway to Denver we were confronted by four Indians afoot. They were about a hundred yards off, lined up four abreast. We pointed our rifles at them. One spoke a little guttural English, explaining that he wanted powwow. We told him to remain where he was, that if they moved we would open fire on them.

He answered, "If you give us whiskey and food we'll let you pass unharmed. If not, we'll kill you and take your animals and packs."

We fired a few shots into the ground, and they rushed back some distance. We moved past them but kept our eyes on them every minute. We had no fight. They had been bluffing.

When we reached the outskirts of Denver we were amazed at the tents, old shacks, and many brick buildings. People and wagons were everywhere — the makings of a beautiful city.

We replenished our supplies here and headed without delay for Central City. There everything was hustle and bustle. Gold was all a person could hear. We decided, after talking with some miners, to cast our lot in Fairplay, some distance west of Central City. Work was plentiful there, and wages were unbelievable. Like all the others, though, we wanted to pan or dig gold, not toil for another man.

One day, while basking in the fine sunshine on the porch of a saloon, we were approached by an elderly gentleman, who offered us work at high pay. We declined his splendid offer. But then he told us of his problem.

"I've got a mine, but I'm too old to work it alone, and I can't hire anybody. They all want their own diggings."

After a lot of discussion he offered us a 30 percent partnership. We grasped it immediately, as we hadn't invested anything and we had nothing to lose. We built us a one-room shack near the mine. It helped keep out the rain and cold — in that part of the country it was always cold at night.

We worked until about the first of December, and the weather became bitter cold. Mr. Simpson announced he was going east for the winter and made us promise to return in the spring. We promised.

Then we decided to go to Santa Fe, New Mexico. We had earned a little more than $2,000, rich by our standards, and we decided to live like kings during the winter. We packed our animals and headed south for Trinidad, Colorado. The going was tough, due to the weather. We kept away from the mountains and traveled in open country.

Many men had been waylaid and robbed of their money in this area, so we took no chances.

About ten miles north of Trinidad we stopped at a mining community to purchase whiskey. I left Ellis with the horses — a man couldn't take his eyes off his horse; if he did it was apt to be stolen. As he waited, a voice from behind him ordered him to drop his lines.

"Don't make a move or I'll put a bullet in you?'

Another man ran and grabbed the lines. When I got the whiskey, nature called me, and I went out the back way. I returned around the building rather than going through the saloon. As I reached the front corner I heard a voice telling Ellis to back up. I drew my revolver just as the man turned my way.

He had evidently figured I would come out the front of the saloon and he would corral me also. The light from the front door exposed him more than it did me. As he raised his rifle on me, I fired. The slug struck him in the chest. I could see the blood as he fell.

Ellis jerked his revolver and fired at the

54

man who held the lines. That man hit for the brush across the road. I looked at the man I had shot and saw that he was a Mexican, stone dead. Men began pouring from the saloon. We fired a few shots into the porch, and they scattered.

We mounted and rode out. About ten miles south and almost into Trinidad we discovered we were being followed. We waited until our pursuers were about a hundred yards from us, then we opened fire on them. We saw no more of them and rode on.

We remained in Trinidad just long enough to buy supplies, then headed over the pass to Raton, New Mexico, and from there headed south for Santa Fe. We were compelled to travel rather slowly because of our heavily loaded packhorse. Two days out of Raton we made camp for the night. We were gathering fuel for the fire when we spotted two Indians looking us over. A few miles back we had seen a wagon headed in this direction, containing a man, woman, and two children. We decided to ride back and make certain that they were all right. The two Indians vanished when they found we had discovered them, and this wagon would be an easier mark for them.

We found the family in good order, and they weren't frightened. They had seen the Indians, and the man declared that he had a good shotgun. Nevertheless, we decided to spend the night with them. We figured if we left them the two bucks might attack.

After dark Ellis suggested we had better go back a piece and watch the road, because those two weren't through by any means. We walked back to a rise and surveyed the area as best we could. The night was light, and we could see for some distance. Soon we saw the two bucks headed toward the wagon, crouched and running from bush to bush. They evidently thought we had ridden off.

When they moved into the road we followed. As they neared the wagon we opened up on them. We loved to shoot those repeating Winchesters. We discovered later that we killed one and wounded the other. The wounded one started running as fast as he could, but

I overtook him and killed him. The man in the wagon and his wife were now convinced, and it scared them out of their wits. We had dragged the bodies of the two bucks out where they could see them. If this may seem rather cruel, consider what would have happened to that family had we not been there. We remained with these people until we came to a village, and headed on to Santa Fe.

We found Santa Fe a wild, wide-open town with very little law supervision. We rented a small adobe house and hired a Mexican who lived next door to guard our belongings, mostly our horses. We spent more time in the saloons than we did in the house.

Before spring we had built ourselves an unfavorable reputation as fighters. One thing in our favor — we were always together. This kept some man from sticking one of us in the back while in a brawl. I relate these stories of our activities so as not to give the impression that we were trying to live like saints. I do maintain that we kept ourselves honest. We refused crooked deals men propositioned to us many times.

When spring arrived we returned to Fairplay. To our surprise we found our claim being worked by strangers. They maintained they had purchased the claim from Mr. Simpson. This didn't sound like the Simpson we knew, so we hired a lawyer to investigate. No record of such a transaction could be found. With the aid of friends, we took the case to court and proved our ownership. The two characters refused to move off the claim. We had to throw them off bodily.

Later these two were corralled with a rope when it was discovered they had murdered Simpson. Each tried to lay the blame on the other. Claim jumping was a serious matter, and so was murder. They were placed in jail at Fairplay and killed while trying to escape. This was mountain justice. To save expenses they had been allowed to try to escape.

We worked this claim for three years. Rather, when we became broke we worked it until we had a stake, and then we'd celebrate until our money was gone. We could have gone home rich men had we used our heads for something more than a hat rack.

We finally sold out to a Kansas City mining company for the paltry sum of $4,000, a fraction of what it was worth. We returned to Santa Fe and were soon broke, for the gaming tables had taken us good. We worked at different jobs to keep going — unsuitable jobs, always looking for another streak of luck.

A saloonkeeper hired Ellis and me to keep down trouble in his place. Law had moved into Santa Fe, and many saloons were closed because of killings, which were becoming too common. All we had to do was sit at a table when one of the riffraff showed, ask him to leave, and if he refused, he was thrown out bodily. The job paid fairly well, and after a few weeks we had only a few rough customers. If a man came in armed, as most men did, we asked him to take off his guns or leave. This usually worked.

One night a man we knew slightly came into the saloon. He was loaded with gold dust and proceeded to get every man in the place drunk. We were all excited, because raw gold was not common in this area. Finally, Ellis and

I got the chance to talk with him, and he gave us the exact location of the gold.

Bright and early the next morning we packed up and set out for the location he had told us about. The place was about fifty miles east of Santa Fe. We made camp at the end of the first day, at dusk. Before we had a chance to unpack, we were attacked by a band of Apaches. We didn't have a chance to make a fight. We mounted in a hurry and made a run for it. We could have easily outrun them if it hadn't been that Ellis's horse was shot from under him. He was taken captive. I watched from a distance to see what they were going to do with him.

Two bucks were dispatched to do me in. I sat my horse and watched them as they came at a dead run. When they were about a hundred yards off, I opened up with my Winchester. I killed one and set the other afoot. Before I could run him down, he was taken by others who had ridden up. I followed them at a safe distance, but when darkness set in they lost me. I rode the trails for two weeks without locating an Apache camp. I thought perhaps I could make a deal

60

with them if they were holding Ellis for ransom, a practice that was becoming quite common.

One day, while riding along and looking over my shoulder quite often, as all riders do in this country, I saw dust behind me and pulled in off the trail to see what was up.

Finally, two Apaches came into view. I decided to let them pass and follow them. Perhaps they would lead me to their camp, where Ellis might be held if they hadn't already killed him. But when they passed I saw a ten-year-old white girl mounted behind one of the bucks. This changed the picture entirely.

I had my rifle and was taking aim at the one with the girl when my horse snorted at the smell of Apaches. Both Indians stopped and sat stock still and listened and looked. I aimed right at the buck's ear and pulled the trigger. He fell dead, and the other escaped. I yelled at the girl not to run, that I was her friend, but she ran like a deer.

Right then I came closer to my Maker than at any other time since leaving home. The buck had run behind a rock. I pulled my revolver and cautiously approached. Quick as lightning he stepped from behind the rock and threw a hatchet at me. It came so close to my head it drew blood. I immediately shot him to death. I retrieved the hatchet and found it a home hand ax, as sharp as a razor.

I then rode to the child, who by that time was sitting on a rock, weeping as though her heart was broken. I took her in my arms and talked quietly to her, and finally she told me that her folks were waiting for her in Santa Fe. She had come west with a family of friends. The Indians had killed that family and burned their wagon and had taken her captive. I assured her that she would be taken to her folks.

I took her to a ranch owned by a man named Jarvis and turned her over to Mrs. Jarvis. Jarvis I knew to be an Indian trader and a coward. He became very upset and asked why I had brought her to them. He said he was on good terms with those Apaches and that when they found those two bodies on the trail they were sure to come to him. He said I'd easily be tracked here. I told him what I expected of him, and said if he didn't carry out my orders I'd return and kill him.

"When those Indians come," I said, "you tell them I rode in, got some food, and left. I'll leave a plain trail for them to follow. And if you say one word about the child, I'll return and nail your cowardly skin to that barn."

I rode off some distance and hid in the bush. I hadn't long to wait. As he suspected, the Apaches rode in, then set out after me. I rode into the rocky country and lost them. Why they gave up the search for me still has me wondering. They are the greatest trackers in the world.

I followed them to their camp and hid out and watched them for two days — for what I didn't know. But soon I made up my mind. On the third day they rode out on a foray, leaving some old men in the camp. I wanted to capture a squaw or a young boy. Soon some boys came near, playing some sort of a game. When one got away from the rest I rode him down and grabbed him by his filthy hair. I threw him to the ground with my knife at his throat.

"Be quiet," I said in Spanish, "or I'll cut off your head."

He was about twelve years old and frightened out of his wits. I asked him if they were holding a white man in the camp. After I pecked him with the knife, he nodded his head. I told him if he did as I told him he would not be harmed — otherwise, I would cut off his arms and legs and carry them away. Indians, especially Apaches, believed that if they were not buried in one piece they would never reach the happy hunting grounds.

"Call one of your friends and tell him I am holding you captive. Tell them to get two old unarmed men to fetch the white man or they'll never see you again."

I had no alternative. It might work, and I had to try something. Soon I saw two old men bringing the worst-looking white man I'd ever laid eyes on. I had to take a close look to recognize Ellis — long hair, long beard, and filthy, dirty, half-starved, his clothing in shreds.

I ordered them to turn him loose. When I had him mounted behind me, I cut the lad loose and we rode off. They stood and watched us ride away. I took Ellis to an honest trader I knew, where he bathed in the river, shaved, cut his hair, and dressed in clean clothing. We camped at a safe spot near the post and talked for hours on end. Nearby was a detachment of cavalry, so we had nothing to fear.

Finally Ellis said, "John, I am ready to return home. I have had enough of this horrible place, but you do as you wish. I will not try to influence you."

We had been in the West nearly six years, and the only thing we had to show for our time was a bad reputation. Back home we could live this down in time.

The worst, however, was yet to come. The night before we left I won heavily in a poker game and split the money with Ellis. This would take us through in style. It was actually the first time we had won since coming west. Since we had sold our possessions, we bought fare on a stage to Raton, New Mexico. Before the stage left we were joined by a lady and her six-year-old daughter. While talking she expressed an insane fear of being taken captive. We assured her that we were both well armed, as were the guards, and that her fears were unfounded. She felt better after this and talked freely.

We left Santa Fe and settled back in our seats. We knew this road and knew we were in for a long, tiresome trip.

★ ★ ★

A well-drawn stage could usually outrun Indians. The trouble was that these Apaches were more cunning than most Indians. Indians would usually ride in behind a stage and kill those on top. Most of the Indians were poorly armed and their horses in poor shape. The guard and the driver were armed with Winchesters and were crack shots.

At dusk of the second day the driver made a terrible mistake. All aboard got down to stretch their legs. One lady had taken a little girl behind the bushes. We were definitely not on the alert, none of us — not that it would have helped if we had been.

Ellis and I were sitting on the ground. The driver was looking after the horses.

Then it happened. From out of nowhere we were surrounded by yelling Apaches. Had we been in the open and had we seen them coming, we might have had a chance to fight them off. As it was, we had no chance whatsoever.

We were knocked to the ground and stripped of everything we had except our clothing. They dragged the two men off the stage and murdered them. They searched the coach, and a yell went up. They had found gold on the stage that we knew nothing about. They also knew they could buy anything they wanted with this yellow stuff. They cut loose the stage horses and ordered us to mount. I took the little girl behind me, and Ellis took the lady.

Soon the lady became hysterical and let out screams that could be heard a mile away. Ellis told her that if she didn't control herself the Indians would kill her and the little girl. She tried desperately to control her emotions and did, to some extent. Now she only sobbed and shook like a leaf in the wind. What a hell of a mess we had gotten ourselves into! We had walked blindly into a trap. We

67

should have ridden our horses.

They boy who led these raiders was a fine specimen of humanity, about six feet in height and weighing about a hundred and eighty pounds. He looked half Mexican, which he proved to be. This young chief rode back and asked if I spoke Mexican. I told him I did fairly well.

He said, "Tell the lady we are not going to harm her. She is to be held for ransom."

I knew she was on her way to join her husband, a cavalry officer at Fort Union. I told her, and it helped some, but she was still frightened so much that she couldn't utter a word.

On the way the young chief stopped at a trading post and bought whiskey. When the lady implored the trader to aid us, he only laughed and said, "You'll be well taken care of. Don't worry." I made a vow to myself to come back here and kill that S.O.B. if I lived.

That night we camped near a fine stream. The Indians killed a deer and gave us a piece, and we roasted it over a fire. The lady refused to touch it, but the little girl ate some. She was too young to realize the seriousness of the situation.

The Indians danced and sang all night long until they became so worn out that they fell asleep — all except the young chief.

During the celebration some of the Indians suggested that they bring out the lady and make her dance. The chief jumped up and grabbed a young buck by the hair and said, "No harm is to come to her, by orders of my father. If any man touches her, I will cut off his head."

The next day about noon we rode into the main Apache camp. It was small, harboring about seventy-five people in all. I was immediately escorted to Chief Great Bull, who looked at me and grinned from ear to ear.

Then, turning to his son, he said, "I know this man. He made me a fine deal in Mexican cows some time back."

I had sold no cows, nor had I been in Mexico, but I kept still. He seemed pleased.

Young Bull brought me pencil and paper. (Though I have been informed that lead did not exist at that time, it did. It was the first I had seen.) I wrote as he suggested to the commanding officer of a cavalry outfit somewhere not too far away. I said that the Apaches were holding the woman and child unharmed. They wanted some cows and horses for their safe return, and I gave our location as well as possible. The wise old chief anticipated this and moved the entire camp.

While in his presence I asked that we be allowed to milk one of his cows for the child and to cook our own meat.

He grinned and said in Mexican, "White people are weak?"

To my amazement he then fetched out an old shotgun and twelve shells.

He said, "This is mine old lady's gun. You may shoot rabbits, but not Indians.

I assured him we would not shoot Indians and thanked him for his hospitality. I went hunting and killed a badger, which was better than nothing. I also milked a cow for the little girl. When the food was ready, we ate like hogs, except the lady and the little girl — they ate sparingly.

I will try to describe this camp. It was stretched along a fine creek. The area was filthy with half-rotted meat and bones, old skins, and rags. It was a horrible mess. We were not exactly unaccustomed to this. The lady, however, had never witnessed such a place, and wondered aloud how they ever managed to survive. The Indians were as filthy as the area, in dirty, ragged clothing, filthy hair and body, except Young Bull, who went about fairly clean. Their homes consisted of poles covered with animal skins, which kept out nothing except the sunshine.

When they cooked their meat — and that's about all they ate — they would kill a beef for the whole camp, and it would lie for days before it was consumed. They gave us two miners' tents to live in. We moved out of camp to near the stream and so got away from most of the terrible odor. The soldiers arrived several days later with horses and cows. Great Bull was disappointed. At first he refused to let the lady and the child go. After a few minutes' consultation with his son, he allowed them to leave. He told the soldiers to bring more to ransom Ellis and me.

Two weeks later a man, woman, and child were brought in and turned over to us to care for. The man went wild. He cursed the Indians, Ellis, and me, and finally had to be subdued. Great Bull sent for me and had me write another note, asking for the same as before. This time, instead of bringing cows and horses, the soldiers raided the camp, killing several Indians and rescuing the captives.

Great Bull accused me of writing the wrong note. He took the shotgun and restricted us to the main camp. If it had not been for his son coming to our rescue, we'd have been killed. Later four soldiers were brought in and tied to posts in the center of the village. We tried to talk to them, but they spat on us and called us every vile name they could muster, including renegades. They said we were working with the Indians, as proved by the notes we had written. We were fully aware now that the army would never ransom us. We were branded as the lowest in the West — renegades, men who sold whiskey and guns to the Indians and planned raids for them. How could we ever convince anyone that we were not guilty?

I wrote a note for the soldiers, and in a few days they were ransomed. But Ellis and I remained. Some time later a celebration was ordered by Great Bull, prior to their going on a raid. The warriors got drunk and yelled and screamed most of the night. The young bucks, to prove their worth, played all sorts of games, such as throwing knives at each other. They were supposed to catch the knives. Some did and some didn't and were badly cut. This night the supreme test was placed in effect — a live rattlesnake was brought in. They were to toss the snake from one to another. The trick was to catch it without being bitten. Young Bull, son of the chief, was bitten on the arm. He ran to us for help. He didn't have much faith in the medicine man. We made a slit in his arm and took turns sucking out the blood. This was the only cure we knew of.

He developed a high fever, and his arm swelled to the size of a stovepipe.

We covered him and told him to try to sleep, that he was going to be all right if he lived, as we were sure he would. This could be our salvation. The Indians looked at us in awe. They felt sure we would drop dead from the poison. When we didn't, they were certain the Great Spirit had shown us special favor. The next morning the young chief's swelling had gone down some, and his fever left. His mother had sat with him all night long and was certain we had saved his life. His father was also pleased and gave us back our shotgun and permission to hunt within reason and to move our tent back near the creek.

People have asked us over the years why we didn't sneak out and escape during the night. The horses were kept under guard, and we had not the slightest idea which way to go. All we could see in all directions was desert, and had we tried, we'd have been tracked down in a couple of hours.

We were in rags. We asked Young Bull for some clothing, and he gave us some bloody army clothes. We took these to the creek, laid them on a rock, and pounded them with another rock until they came clean. That was a practice we had learned from the Indians. From then on we were never mistreated, though we were aware that they might turn on us at any time if something went wrong. We didn't like the idea of wearing these clothes, but we had no alternative. If the army had caught us in these uniforms, we'd have been shot on the spot. We found out later the things that caused the army to brand us as renegades — the notes and the wearing of army uniforms, a common practice among the Apaches.

The Indians were fascinated by this writing of notes. Great Bull was afraid we'd escape, and he would then have no one to carry out this note business. He directed us to teach Young Bull to write. Young Bull reported for his first lesson. He had been in a Spanish mission until he was ten years old and had learned to write some in Spanish, admittedly not much. An hour later Great Bull showed up and asked Young Bull to write for him. When his son explained that learning to write would take some time, the chief called off the lessons. If a man could not learn to write in an hour, there was something wrong with him.

One day two Indian scouts for the army called on Great Bull. These men worked both sides. They kept the Indians informed of army activities and the army informed of what the Indians were about. Now and then one of these traitors would be burned at the stake. Still, their work went on. Geronimo was captured by this treasonable act — his own people sold him out for a price.

The scouts reported that there was no soldier activity in the area that Great Bull planned to move through to his winter quarters. Here is something I have never been able to understand — why he moved his camp to this higher altitude with a colder climate. It was much warmer in the desert where we were. The move required about ten days. The process was slow since the squaws had to walk. The chief ordered the move ahead of time so that several raids could be executed for winter food.

Young Bull kept us in front of the rest, and the warriors were spread out to ward off an attack by other tribes. All these small tribes were at war with each other. They would capture each other's women and children and hold them for ransom along with whites now and then. If they were not ransomed, they were made slaves.

When we came in sight of the mountains, Young Bull pointed out the place where they meant to winter. It was situated on a high plateau. Behind this plateau were cliffs about five hundred feet in height. This plateau could be reached only by a narrow path and only on foot. We climbed to the plateau and found it to be about a mile wide and about two miles long. A stream ran through this area from one end to the other. The plateau was almost inaccessible except from the east. Enemies could be held off by rolling rocks down this trail. We could tell by the accumulated filth we found there that they had been using this place for a long time.

North of this plateau, on a level with the desert, there was a beautiful valley about the same size as the plateau and covered with trees and green grass. There was an old, deserted mining camp in evidence there.

Ellis asked me, "Why the hell didn't they move into this valley?"

I told him, "Your guess is as good as mine."

The whole thing was unreasonable. In this valley the Apaches kept their livestock well guarded at all times. We asked Young Bull to let us live in the valley and guard the stock. He refused. He knew we would leave if we got hold of a horse.

The Indians built their homes along the creek out of sticks covered with skins, with a hole in the top to let smoke escape. When the wind was right, the smoke ran them out. They could have built houses of logs except that this work was too heavy for the squaws, who did all the home chores.

We decided to build our home in a cave. We dug a cave back in the bank about twelve feet long and eight feet wide. We propped this as we had done the mine at Fairplay. The ceiling was made from strong poles placed close together. We made certain, by propping the cave with heavy timbers, that it wouldn't cave in during the winter whenever a fire was built.

In the valley at the old mining camp we found a small boiler and some tin. We made a stove of this boiler and a stovepipe from the rusted tin. This we poked out through the roof. The entrance was made of poles covered with skin. We were quite comfortable in this place, considering everything. The fire would give off enough light for us to move about with ease. We built our beds of poles laid horizontally, one on each side of the stove.

Shortly after we arrived, the chief ordered a raid. One morning they pulled out, leaving us with the women and a few older men. We decided to go to the valley, kill a couple of Indians, and escape. But when we reached the valley, we found it far too well guarded and had to dismiss this plan immediately. We climbed to a high peak and surveyed the west with an escape plan in mind. As far as we could see there were only high mountains confronting us.

When the raiders returned, they were

a sorry sight to behold. Many had been killed, including Great Bull, and many had been wounded. Young Bull told us they had run into soldiers and ranchers and had brought back nothing but trouble. He called the Indians together and announced that he would lead them in his father's place. He would be their chief. There was some grumbling, but he had enough power to make his decision stick. From here on he was officially the chief.

He changed his name to Black Cloud in order to avoid the evil spirit, who, for some unknown reason, had cast a bad spell on him. His being the chief pleased us considerably. Had some other man been appointed, we might have been done away with. But we had once saved the young chief's life, and he would remember this.

Things were quiet at first, then winter set in with all its fury. We had killed several head of deer and had them hidden away from the Indians. Otherwise they would have taken them for their own use. How we wished for a deck of cards! Although they had been our ruination, we could have passed the dull hours much more easily if we'd had them.

About the first of February Black Cloud paid us a visit in our cave. He was more intelligent than most Indians in that he wasn't above taking advice from us. He told us that his people were starving and that he refused to let them eat their horses. He said he wanted to go on a raid, only after the last one he feared for his warriors.

I figured he still had the gold he had taken from the stage when he attacked us, and suggested he use this to buy cattle.

He laughed and said, "No white man would sell an Apache anything. They'd only kill him and take the gold."

Then a thought came to him.

I was called Wild Jack by the Indians, and now Black Cloud said, "You Wild Jack! Take the gold and buy cows. If you, do not return I will kill Williams — he will be held here."

It was shrewd thinking on his part. So it was planned that I go, and I willingly accepted the plan. I took with me several strips of dried beef. Black Cloud gave me roughly $1,500 worth of gold. He had no idea of the value of this dust.

The weather was bitter cold. I wrapped up the best I could and still ride. My boots were long since gone, and I wrapped my feet in deerskin. Down in the valley I picked a fine horse and roped him. At daybreak I was off, having bade Ellis farewell and told him I'd return as soon as possible. We wished each other luck, and I was off to the south, as suggested by Black Cloud.

I faced a fine mist of snow. Every now and then I'd stop and jump up and down and wave my arms to keep from freezing. Had I met anyone, they'd have begun shooting at first sight! My hair was long, as was my beard; my clothing hung in tatters under an old, worn-out army overcoat. And I was filthy dirty. I carried a revolver and several rounds of ammunition. I couldn't have fired had I wanted to, my hands were so stiff from the cold.

When night fell I saw a house in the distance. I was afraid to approach it in my condition and in the darkness. I found a haystack surrounded by a high fence to keep out stock. I got the gate open and led my horse inside, removed his bridle so that he could eat, and crawled into the hay and was soon asleep.

I was rudely awakened by a voice calling for me to come out. When the man saw me, he backed off. No doubt he had never seen a human who looked as bad as I did. He demanded to know what the hell I was doing, feeding my horse his hay. While we talked I jumped and waved my arms for circulation. I knew I might have to shoot him and had to be able to use my hands.

I told him I was a prospector and had lost my supplies to Indians. I told him I had a little gold and would pay him for the trouble I had caused. He softened when he saw the gold. I poured a little into his hat and promised to stop on my way back. This seemed to please him, and he allowed me to leave, I was glad to get away from him, for I figured he couldn't be trusted.

That afternoon I came to a house and was so miserable that I just rode up and yelled. Two men came out with rifles, and one asked, "What are you?"

I gave them the same story I had given the other man. One took my horse to the stable, and the other led me to a cabin where there was a hot fire in a stove. After he fed me, he wanted to hear my story. Since he looked like a man who could be trusted, I told him I had come to buy cattle and supplies, that I could pay in gold. He was extremely pleased at the prospect of selling a hundred cattle in the dead of winter. I told him I wanted to go to a town to buy other things I needed.

He said, "Under the circumstances, and considering your appearance, maybe you ought to let me send a man in your stead. He can buy whatever you want."

To this plan I readily agreed, and made out a list of what ought to be bought for me: one tin pot, two tin cups, several cans of salve for lice, heavy coats for Ellis and me, a pair of boots for each of us, a can or sack of coffee, and other things I can't recall. Last but not least, six bottles of whiskey and a deck of cards.

The man took a pack horse with him. He needed it for all I wanted. I also bought a horse from the rancher. I told him I wanted the cattle turned loose in the valley near the plateau, and he said he'd give me enough men to get them there. All I had to do was lead the way.

By the time the man got back with my supplies, the cattle were bunched and ready to move out. He sent a chuck wagon and four riders. We had a little trouble getting the cattle started, but were soon under way. After the better part of three days we sighted the plateau. I knew we had been scouted, for not a wisp of smoke showed from the Indians' camp. We drove the cattle into the valley, and, after handshaking all around, the riders departed.

As soon as they were well out of sight, the Indians came rolling off that hill like so much water. When I met Ellis we embraced. It had been a hell of an undertaking, but we had made it. We enlisted the aid of two youngsters to carry our supplies to our cave. The other Indians were far too busy to bother about what we had in those bags. They began killing cattle as though they were mad. An Indian celebration was held that night, and it lasted a long time.

I had been given about $1,500 in gold, and had spent about half that amount. The rest I socked away for Ellis and me if we should ever escape. The whiskey we buried. If the Indians had known we had it, it wouldn't have lasted a minute.

Ellis and I made coffee, poured whiskey into it, and got a bit drunk ourselves. The next day was clean-up time. We cut each other's hair and beard, carried water and took baths. We rubbed lice salve on our bodies and put on fresh clothing. Again we felt like men. We had been pretty low prior to this. Black Cloud came to the cave to express his appreciation, and we gave him a bottle of whiskey after he promised not to reveal it to the others.

Among the supplies was a deck of cards, and we played cards until we became sick of them. I have been asked why we weren't forced to work. By now we had been taken into the tribe and enjoyed the same privileges as the male Indians. The women did the work. The men did the fighting and brought in the food.

At long last spring came in all its glory. How we had managed to exist through that winter is beyond my comprehension. How we kept from going stark raving mad only God knows.

The Indians were making preparations to return to the desert. Why they wanted to live in the desert in summer rather than in this mountain place was incomprehensible. On the day Black Cloud announced they were moving, Indians carried down the hazardous trail all their belongings. When they set out, the squaws, as usual, were walking.

One day the inevitable came. Black Cloud called to us and pointed out four wagons crossing some distance away. He was delighted, for he and his followers loved to raid such a helpless train. There would be rich looting, and they would gain several horses and cows.

We told him that it was not far to the cavalry camp.

"If you raid those wagons, they'll have the soldiers down on us before you can get the women and children to safety."

He considered this for some time, then

ordered the braves to let the wagons pass unmolested.

Finally camp was made near a stream on high ground as before, though not in the same place. They put up a few lodges, and most of the Indians cast their lot on the ground. We built our lean-to off the ground away from rattlesnakes and away from the others.

Ellis said to me, "John, we have to get out of this camp. We have to escape."

And he was right. We had to chance the desert and would the next time the Apaches should go on a raid. We were living on borrowed time with these warriors. Any time they might kill us.

One night Black Cloud announced that they were going on a raid. Every available man would go. The extra horses were moved to an undisclosed spot. When we couldn't find the horses, we decided to go on foot. It was either get out or die in the attempt. We figured the raiders would not return for two or three days. With a little luck, we could be well on our way by that time.

Black Cloud's mother suspected what we were up to. She fetched us two bags of gold and pointed out the way, a high peak about fifty miles off.

"Keep your eye on that peak," she said. "Go and don't look back."

When we were off a way, she called, "And may the Great Spirit show you special favor."

We took the shotgun and five rounds of ammunition, a knife, several strips of dried beef, and two canteens of water. These canteens each held about a half gallon of water.

We set out heading south, as she had directed, and toward the peak. We soon found just how soft we were. The sun was blistering hot. There was no shade, and the sand caused us to slip as on fresh fallen snow.

We kept a slow pace. We wanted to put as much distance as possible between ourselves and the camp. After we had run out of water, we were lucky to come to a small stream. Our feet were blistered, our eyes swollen around the rims. We slept that night on the sand. At daylight we were off again. We would walk awhile and rest awhile. We stuck to a ridge from where we could constantly see the peak the squaw had indicated.

That afternoon we ran out of water again, and by darkness our tongues and our lips were swollen. We had fallen to the sand when we saw several head of deer heading south.

Ellis said, "They are heading for water!"

We followed them and soon came to a spring. This water was cool and surrounded by small trees. We drank and bathed our tired aching bodies, then rested. Here we discarded our boots, for our feet were so blistered we couldn't keep them on.

The next morning we went into the water, clothes and all. We figured this would help for awhile, and it did, but we dried out very soon. We walked all of that day. That night we reached a deserted homestead. We drank water from the well and bathed as best we could. We knew the dangers of drinking bad water but took the chance. We killed a young calf and roasted some of it. We couldn't eat more than a small amount of it, for it made us sick to our stomachs.

The next morning we found out how

badly we were spent. We could barely walk. We would walk for a while, then lie full length on the sand. All that day we staggered a few feet, then fell to the sand. Our eyes were so swollen we had to pry them open to see. About dusk we were resting, and I saw something that resembled a fence. It was on top of a rise.

I got Ellis to his feet, and we staggered to the top of this rise and came to a well-traveled road. Before long I made out lights in the distance. We staggered toward them. Then we heard horses coming and hid in a ditch. We knew we had to use our heads and not rush into anything. The riders proved to be cavalry, and we remained in hiding until they had passed. We knew it was an army camp ahead. We also knew that we couldn't go in, but perhaps we could steal some food and water there.

Ellis said, "I'll go in for water, so you wait."

He returned with a canteen filled from the trough. Nevertheless, it was water. We slept soundly until daybreak.

When Ellis shook me awake, he said,

"That's a trading post and not an army camp."

I bathed my eyes and looked. He was correct.

Closer observation revealed this to be the place the Indians had passed when we had the lady and child with us. The man inside would be the man I promised myself to kill if I escaped, many months past. We approached cautiously. We figured he had been warned by the Indians of our coming. Anyway, the dogs soon gave us away, and the man I remembered came out with a rifle.

I pulled the shotgun on him and warned him not to move.

He said, "I don't mean to harm you, but I thought at first you were skulkers."

He took us inside and fed us soup, and after a few drinks of whiskey we felt considerably better. We told him we wanted two rifles, ammunition, two horses and saddles, and certain supplies, that we had the gold to pay him with. He seemed a little reluctant, and I had to tell him to get a move on or I'd gladly blow out his brains and take what we wanted.

We carried our supplies to the barn to rest. We couldn't go on in our condition.

Ellis told the man, "We are going to sleep one at a time. If anybody bothers us we'll gladly shoot him."

He replied, "Don't worry. Nobody knows you're here."

The third day I was in the store and asked, "Have you heard from the Apaches?"

He said, "Not a word."

He had a twelve-year-old boy whom he kept perched on top of a hill to watch for dust clouds.

While I was there the boy came in and said, "Big dust cloud, that way," and he pointed North.

The trader grabbed his glasses and rushed to the hilltop. As soon as he had left the boy began grabbing food and stuffing it into his mouth as though he was starved. We found out he was a slave, and I made up my mind to help him if possible.

Soon the trader returned all out of breath and said, "You men better pack up and leave. That dust is a band of Apaches."

I hurried and told Ellis. We saddled up and headed out. I knew the man would tell the Apaches about us as soon as they arrived. I wanted to kill him, but that would wait. I couldn't shoot a man in cold blood.

Ellis and I rode to high rocky ground and figured this might throw them off our trail. We rode about ten miles, and our horses began to play out. They were of a poor breed and old, and we had no chance of outrunning the Indians. We decided we would have to make a stand. We led our horses out of sight and took up a position behind the rocks. We had good rifles and plenty of ammunition and should be able to give a good account of ourselves.

We didn't have long to wait. About twenty Apaches rode to within about three hundred yards of our position and stopped to talk.

Ellis said, "John, this is it. Take as many as you can."

No other words were spoken. As we watched, one Indian rode out from the rest and held his rifle over his head, indicating peace. We immediately recognized him as Black Cloud. He rode up in front of us and said, "I followed you across the desert to make sure you did not die. Come out. You are no longer my prisoners. You are free."

I asked him if he would allow us to take the Mexican boy from the trader and find a home for him.

He replied, "Yes, after I kill the trader. I want the boy to see him die."

We followed the Indians back to the trading post. Black Cloud called for the trader to come out and shot him to death as he stepped through the door.

He told us to go to the corral and pick three good horses, and he gave the boy a small sack of gold.

He said, "Take the boy to the San Juan mission where I was raised. They'll take him in."

He held his rifle up in salute and rode back to the trading post. We watched as the Indians piled everything they wanted onto two wagons from the store. Then they set the place afire.

We headed east to find San Juan, which Black Cloud had said was to the east in Texas. The mission gladly took in the boy, and we remained there for a week. All rested up, we headed for home. By horseback, stage, and train we made it in good order.

At first we were shunned by our old friends. But time heals all wounds. They got over their blame of us, and the government forgave us for whatever charges they had against us. We both married and raised large families. Our farms are side by side, near Greenview, Illinois.

Postscript: John Blane died in 1906, and Ellis Williams died in 1910. They are buried side by side in a beautiful little cemetery at Sweet Water Illinois. John Blane in 1974 had three living near-relatives: myself of Leavenworth, Kansas; Mable Stephens of Canon City, Colorado; and May Miller of Greenview, Illinois. Of the Williams family there is no information. — W.M.

Doc Holliday and Santa Fe

WHEN John Montgomery and Coyote Smith parted company after their two years of prospecting, John hunted buffalo and drove teams for a freighting company. This took him to all parts of the West. Among them was Santa Fe, New Mexico Territory. He was so impressed that he later moved there and bought out a livery stable. Thereby he made the acquaintance of one of the most colorful and controversial figures of the Old Frontier.

Doc Holliday arrived in Santa Fe with a great big wild-looking character called Pole Cat Adams. Pole Cat told Montgomery that Doc had hired him to take care of his stock (three horses) and to do the camp chores, since Doc refused to belittle himself by performing such menial tasks. Doc kept his horses at Montgomery's stable, and Pole Cat was responsible for their safety. He said that Doc had killed a gambler in Texas and been ordered to leave town. He hired Adams to go along with him to Santa Fe.

On their way, as they were making camp one night, two trail-weary characters rode in and announced they were taking Doc's horses. Assuming from Doc's black clothing and sombre mien that he was a preacher and that Adams was unarmed, these strangers thought they had nothing to fear. That Doc wore a gun on his hip was natural, even for a preacher, in these parts. They did not know he also had one under his coat. They made him give up the hip gun, but didn't suspect the other. One went through Doc's supplies and found a bottle of whiskey while his companion pointed a rifle at them from his horse. Doc said nothing. The man on the ground took a long pull at Doc's bottle, turned his back to Doc to hand it to his pal in the saddle, who tipped it skyward, taking his eyes off Doc. Within a second Doc went into action. He shot the man on the horse through the middle and, when he fell from the horse still moving, shot him again to make sure. The one on the ground he shot through the head. He had Adams drag the bodies into the brush and search them for money. There was almost $400 on them. Doc split it with Adams. He took their horses, which were healthy and strong, and turned his own worn-out ones loose.

"We'd better move on," he told Adams, "because those two bastards either robbed a bank or a stage, and somebody will be looking for them." Where else could they head but west?

In one of their campfire talks en route, Doc philosophized: "I always live by my wits. I let the other man make a mistake. I never rush things. I'm not in the habit of robbing dead men, but why leave the loot for someone else to find?"

At Mesa, Texas, Doc got into a poker game and, as usual, soon won heavily. He told the others he had to go for some rest, but would return and continue the game.

"You're not goin' anywhere, Doc," they said. "You're goin' to give us a

99

chance to get even right now."

Doc was ready for them. He had already instructed Adams to have the horses at the front of the saloon. He pulled out his pistol and told his challengers he'd put a bullet through the first man that moved. As he was backing out of the saloon the fat bartender came toward him with a shotgun. Doc shot him down, made a quick exit, jumped into the saddle of one of the waiting horses, and, with Adams, rode east, the direction they had come from.

"Where the hell are you going?" Adams asked, once they were safely away. "We've just come from that direction."

Doc answered: "Those men back there believe we are heading for Santa Fe, so they'll hunt for us in that direction. Later we'll turn north, then back west. Never do what a man thinks you'll do. Take advantage of him and you'll win. If we'd headed west, they'd have overtaken us in no time. By circling back and around, we'll be in Santa Fe while they're still wondering where the hell we are."

They made it, of course, to Santa Fe without mishap. Adams put up the animals, and Doc began gambling, as was his habit.

They had been in town for a week when a young man accosted them on the street and asked Doc, "Are you Holliday?"

Doc replied that he was.

"I have reason to believe you killed my two brothers," the young man accused him.

"I killed a couple of men who tried to rob me back in Texas," Doc freely admitted. "About their relationship to you I don't know."

"I just wanted to hear you say so, because I don't want to kill an innocent man. Now, you dirty little dried-up bastard, I'm going to kill you, so get ready to die."

He jerked out his gun. Before he could use it Doc shot him through the leg. The young man fell to the ground, dropping his gun. Doc walked over to him and said, "You better listen, and damn good. If you ever cross me again I'll put a bullet through your head, and don't forget it."

A number of observers witnessed this affair. Doc was not held, since he had been threatened. The sheriff did tell him to stay out of any more trouble. Doc's reply: "I'll try." But trouble was something he couldn't avoid.

Some time later in a poker game, a gambler named Remick accused Doc of cheating. As Doc started to rise from his chair the man grabbed at him. All he got was Doc's coat. He stepped back when he saw Doc's gun in a shoulder holster and attempted to draw his own weapon. He was dead from a bullet in his chest when he hit the floor.

Doc was lodged in jail, for Remick was well liked. The sheriff said Doc would have to stand trial. It so happened that a celebration was in progress at the time. The sheriff and his deputies were busy keeping people in order and left the jail unattended. While this was going on Adams dropped by the jail to talk with Doc.

"I'll never get a fair trial," Doc told him. "So hitch a team to the back window and pull it out. Have horses ready, and we'll ride out easily."

The scheme worked as planned. Adams

pulled out the whole back side of the jailhouse.

When they were some way out of town, Doc told Adams he was heading for Kansas, adding, "You're welcome to come along if you like." But Adams had a good reason for not going to Kansas. "They have a murder warrant out for me over there, so I'll stay in this area."

Adams was well compensated by Doc for his part in the jail break. He was less well rewarded by the sheriff of Santa Fe. Upon his return he was jailed for helping Doc escape and sentenced to six months at hard labor. He spent that time building a new rock jail.

Before Doc reached Kansas he had been accused of three killings — one in Raton, one in Durango, one in Denver. All this was related to John Montgomery by Bat Masterson when they met later.

In 1879 Montgomery took his family to Tombstone, Arizona, the town everybody said was too tough to die. He was there in the most crucial years of its dramatic history. The following stories are taken from his diary kept during those years. No previous historian is old enough

103

to have ever talked to any bona fide old Tombstoner who belonged to the period from 1879 to 1883. Much of what has been written on this subject was fabricated by men who hated Wyatt Earp and other lawmen of the Old West. Their imaginations were more vivid than their concern with accuracy.

John Montgomery lived in Tombstone for twenty years. He was eyewitness to the famous fight at the O.K. Corral — perhaps the only eyewitness at the start of that fight. He knew all the contestants — the good and the bad, the lawmen and the outlaws. His trustworthiness is beyond question. His diary is not hearsay. It is an exact account.

Montgomery was not called to testify at Wyatt's trial. For that reason he refused throughout his life to make a public statement about what happened that day. But he recorded every important event of his long years on the frontier. And that was one of them.

Neither was Doc Holliday called to testify. Both men could have sworn without hesitation that Tom McLaury was armed, a much disputed point. But that will come later. From here through Chapter 7 we turn the story over to John Montgomery — quoting from his ledger and other verbatim accounts he left behind.

Introduction to Tombstone — and John Ringo

WE arrived in Tombstone about the middle of May 1879 and camped outside of town to be near water. The next morning I walked in to look over the place. It was early, and the only place open was a saloon. So I stepped inside for a drink. Two men were at the bar — one a tall, fine-looking man, six feet tall and weighing about a hundred and eighty pounds; the other a shorter, desperate-looking character who I later learned was the scum of the earth.

The taller of the two introduced himself as John Ringo; the other was Pony Deal. I explained my business in Tombstone, and Ringo said, "We're in the cattle business," which brought a laugh from all hands. After a few drinks I continued on my way, looking the place over. My first impression of the town was not good.

It was far too early in the morning. By the middle of the afternoon the place became a beehive of activity. The outlaws had begun to move around, and the saloons were all open. The rich ore mined in and around this city amounted to $20,000,000 and drew in men from all walks of life, from honest bankers to the lowest cutthroats on God Almighty's earth.

After a time I set myself up in the horse-trading business. I soon learned that the place was alive with outlaws that killed, robbed, or whatever, and were never brought to trial. They boasted openly of their evil deeds and defied the law. Witnesses were afraid to testify against them for fear of their lives. Murder to them was as normal as sand in the desert. I was compelled to get along with them, since they did business with me. I didn't have to like them. In fact, I hated everyone of them with a passion — except Ringo, who once saved my life. I firmly believe that had it not been for strong drink Ringo would have made a good citizen. When he was drunk, which was most of the time, he was as bad as the others.

I had not been in business more than a few days when Old Man Clanton called on me, introduced himself, and told me he could furnish me with all the horses I needed and also with grain and hay. I did not know then that he was the leader of the outlaw element in Tombstone and the surrounding area.

I'd like to name some of the outlaw scum of Tombstone at this time: Old Man Clanton, Curly Bill [Graham], John Ringo, Pony Deal, Johnny Barnes, Bill Johnson, Ed and Johnny Lyle, Bill Hicks, Milt Hicks, Frank Patterson, Frank Stilwell, Pete Spence, Frank and Tom McLaury, Ike Clanton, Billy Clanton, Billy Clairborne, Joe Hill, Jim Crane, Harry Head. There are many more outlaws, too numerous to mention here.

One time John Ringo came to me and asked me to lend him a hundred dollars. He so impressed me that I loaned him the money. A few days later he repaid me in full, with interest. From then on he visited me quite often, and we would discuss the present situation and the past.

When sober, he represented a fine-looking specimen of humanity. He dressed well, kept his hair trimmed, and was very courteous, especially to the ladies. He would set their hearts aflutter when they'd meet him on the street. He would bow slightly and tip his hat and speak softly to ladies of all walks of life. In extreme contrast, under the influence of strong drink he let himself go. He wouldn't shave, his clothes became soiled, and he was discourteous to all he met. At such a time he became a gutter bum.

Often, when he was trying to get over a prolonged drunk, he would come to my stable and ask if he could sleep in the loft or in my office, to get away from his outlaw friends. On one such occasion he saved my life, and I have always been grateful to him for it.

A harness-maker named Stillings owed me considerable money, which he made no effort to pay. I was compelled to take him to court, where he was directed to pay me in full, and he did. But he had become my bitter enemy. Shortly after the court ruling he came to the stable drunk, called me vile names, then pulled a gun and said he was going to kill me. His shouting awoke Ringo, who was asleep in my office. Ringo walked outside and struck Stillings a blow on the head which knocked him to the ground.

Stillings dropped his gun, and Ringo kicked it to him, saying, "Pick it up. I want to see how you perform against an armed man."

Stillings begged Ringo not to kill him. Ringo told him to take his gun and get out.

"If I ever see you again I'll put a bullet in your head," he added.

As directed, Stillings picked up his gun and started to leave. When he reached the roadway he turned and fired a shot at Ringo. Ringo in turn fired a shot at him. Both missed. Stillings had already stepped around the corner of the building when Ringo fired.

As Ringo started to leave, he said to me, "John, you'd best start packing a pistol. If you don't, one of your friends is likely to kill you, and you'd better get some practice."

I thanked him for what he had done, and he replied, "Forget it, John. I owe you a hell of a lot more."

Some time later, Ringo came to me and told me a story about how he had become involved with a miner's daughter and how she insisted on getting married. Ringo told her he was a no-good outlaw and that sooner or later somebody would kill him. He told me he was actually in love with her but he would no more take her among his friends than he would his mother. He asked my advice.

I told him to marry her take her to some distant city where nobody knew him or her get a decent job, and quit drinking.

He looked steadily at me for a moment and replied, "John, I know you mean well, but I have been a drunk since I was fifteen, and an outlaw for the same length of time. It's too late to change now."

Later Ringo left town for a spell on business. When he returned he found that this girl had married a man by the name of Pool or Poor (I am not certain which). He did nothing at first, but it bothered him. He told me she had married a bastard out of spite.

"He's no good for her. He's not a known outlaw, but he's very friendly with the others."

One day Curly Bill told Ringo that this man was mistreating the girl. Ringo boiled over and rode to the man's ranch. He goaded the man into a fight and killed him. A Mexican tried to come to the man's aid, and Ringo killed him too. This Mexican's wife ran at Ringo with a shotgun, and he killed her.

He ordered one of the Mexicans on the ranch to bury them all, and said, "If you mention one word of this, I'll come back and kill you too."

The girl and Ringo left town for a while. When they returned they were married. They lived together now and then, whenever Ringo was in town. When he was found dead she attended his funeral, then came to visit me. She asked me not to reveal their relationship to anyone. She said she was leaving this godforsaken place and would never return. She also told me that she was pregnant by Ringo.

Years later I looked her up in George Town, Colorado.

She had married a man named Holbrook and had three children, the eldest named John. She told me that this boy would never know that the infamous Ringo was his father. That visit brought back many memories.

When Ringo and the others read of Wyatt Earp's coming [to Tombstone] and of his reputation of being a great lawman and gunfighter Ringo confided in me that the outlaws would kill that S.O.B. before the week was out. They soon found that Earp wasn't easy to kill. Shibell was sheriff of Pima County at the time, and he made Wyatt a deputy sheriff before he reached town.

In 1880, Fred White, ex-army officer and a good man, but not tough enough to handle the Tombstone scum, was appointed City Marshal of Tombstone. When Wyatt Earp arrived, with him was the West's notorious gunslinger Doc Holliday, whom I mentioned before. Later came Big Nose Kate Elder or Fisher as some claimed, an old dancehall girl friend of Doc and a real hell raiser. I later learned her real last name was Horony. Later on I believe she married

113

a man named Cummings.

When Wyatt's brother Virgil arrived in town, Morgan Earp was already on the scene. Wyatt's first assignment was the guarding of the Wells Fargo stages. For some reason, while he rode shotgun in that capacity not one stage was molested.

Note: One fault I find with my grandfather's diary is that he did not keep an exact chronological account as to dates of events. In many cases he waited for some time to pass and then wrote about several past events under one date. He did not realize at the time that in later years this would cause some confusion.
— Wayne Montgomery

Wyatt Earp Comes to Tombstone

IN the fall of 1880 Wyatt Earp went to Tucson on business. When he returned he found the cowboys, as the outlaws were sometimes called, raising hell in town. Deputy Sheriff Behan refused to try and stop them, so Marshal White called in Wyatt Earp. On the street Curly Bill, backed by the Clantons and several others of that kind, pulled a gun on White. Wyatt grabbed Curly Bill while he was shooting White in the body. White died the next day. Curly Bill was not held to account, because the authorities decided it had been an accident.

The others who had been with Curly Bill that night were arrested by Wyatt. Every one of them had to be cracked over the head before submitting to arrest. They were all given a light fine for disturbing the peace.

Later on, when Cochise County was

115

cut out of Pima County, with the county seat at Tombstone, John Behan was appointed sheriff by Governor Fremont until the November elections of 1882. Earp was furious and said he felt he was entitled to the appointment. The people thought Behan was a good choice over Earp, but some said he favored the scum of Tombstone at every chance.

Mattie Moreland said that Doc Holliday wasn't all bad. I knew him well and failed to see any good in him, though it is said that there is some good in all men. Mattie came to Tombstone to go into the ladies' clothing business. After purchasing a small building, she stocked it with the finest of ladies' needs. On the morning she was to open for business she walked briskly to her shop and found a man waiting for her and her building on house jacks. The man told her she hadn't purchased the ground, only the building. He said that if she didnt come up with $300 more they were going to move the building. She tried to reason with this crook, but to no avail. He insisted on getting the money, which she did not have. She had sunk every nickel she

116

owned into this venture.

The only compassion ever displayed by Doc Holliday was for women and children. Bat Masterson told me that Doc had killed three men for mistreating women and children. On this morning Doc was out for an early morning stroll when he came across this lady in distress, weeping bitterly. He pardoned himself to the lady and asked if he could be of any assistance. She looked at Doc and thought him to be a preacher because of his immaculate black clothes. So she unburdened her woes on Doc. Doc asked her to take a walk, as the words he had for this man were not for a lady's ears.

After she left Doc walked over to the man and asked, "You're new in this town, aren't you?"

The man replied that he was. Then Doc tore into him. He called him every vile name in his vast vocabulary of vile words.

"Now," said Doc, "you put that building back exactly as it was when you sold it to her."

To make his point clear, Doc poked a cocked pistol up against the man's nose. The man didn't lose any time, and soon he had the building back in place. Doc sat nearby in a chair to supervise the work. Finally he said, "Get on the next stage out of town. If I ever meet you again I'll put a bullet between your eyes."

The man caught the next stage out, all right, and never returned to Tombstone, according to Mattie Moreland.

[Mattie ran this shop for many years and was never again molested.]

Another story in Doc's favor was related to me by Benito Romero and Doc himself. Doc had a horse go lame on him, and he wanted to buy another horse to ride while the lame one mended. He was advised to ride to a ranch some distance from Tombstone. He bought the horse he wanted and was returning home when he became lost, due to a shortcut he had made. After wandering about for some time he spotted a homesteader's shack and made his way there to ask directions.

Just as he reached the back side of the house he was startled by a blood-curdling scream. He dismounted and cautiously approached the corner of the house and looked around. What he saw caused him to go into immediate action. A lady was standing in the center of the yard, calling to a six-months-old baby off about fifty feet. Every time she started for the baby he crawled closer to two coiled rattlers in the shade of a bush. Rattlers can't take much hot sun, and when the weather becomes hot they spend their time in the shade of a tree or under a rock. Doc took aim, resting his arm against the building, and fired. He hit one snake, then finished off the other. The shots frightened the baby, and he started toward his mother full speed. His mother lay full length on the ground. She had fainted on hearing Doc's shots, for she had not known of his presence.

As Doc stood there holding his pistol in his hand, a man ran out of the house with a cocked shotgun. He took one look at Doc holding a gun in his hand and his wife lying on the ground. Naturally, he thought Doc had shot his wife, and the screaming baby did not help matters any. Had his wife not regained consciousness at that precise moment and yelled at her man, he would have shot Doc. She pointed at the snakes and told him what had transpired.

The man was sorry, and Doc told him, "Forget it. I'd have done the same in your place."

One day Doc came upon two boys engaged in a fist fight, and he broke it up. One boy ran off, but the other picked up a stick and began beating Doc over the head, knocking his new and expensive hat to the ground. Doc tried in vain to stop the lad, who was only about fourteen years old. But he was too much for wizened little Doc. Therefore, to stop him, Doc fired a shot into the ground. The boy, frightened out of his wits, ran home yelling, "He shot me, he shot me!"

The boy's father had Doc arrested, and when they came to court the man claimed that Doc had tried to kill his son. The judge, who knew Doc quite well, told them that Doc was a crack marksman.

"If he had intended to shoot your son, he'd never have missed."

He fined Doc ten dollars for disturbing the peace.

The man was still irate and shouted, "I'm going home and get a shotgun, and I'll come back and fix you good."

Doc told him, "Mister you point a gun at me, and I'll not fire at your feet. I'll put a bullet between your eyes."

The man did not return. Perhaps some kind-hearted person explained to him who Doc was.

When the city passed a law prohibiting the carrying of weapons on the streets of Tombstone, Doc was made an unpaid deputy so that he could carry a gun. Had he appeared on the streets unarmed, he wouldn't have lasted five minutes. When the outlaw scum found out that Doc was permitted to carry a pistol, they cried loud and often. They claimed that Doc was as bad as any of them or worse. Nevertheless, Doc continued to carry his pistol.

The only man on earth that Doc had the least respect for was Wyatt Earp. He promised Wyatt not to get into trouble — why is not clear — and for this reason he did not rid Tombstone of several outlaws by shooting them. But he did run several out of town.

Johnny Tyler a self-proclaimed bad man, once approached Doc and told him, "I know of the bartender you killed at Mesa, Texas, and for a slight consideration I'll gladly keep my mouth shut."

This occurred in a saloon filled with people. Doc called Johnny all his choice vile words, and Johnny, who didn't know Doc too well, cried out, "Let's go outside and fight!"

Doc asked, "What's the matter with right here in the saloon?"

This suited the proud bad man. He backed off and touched a hand to his pistol. He found himself looking into Doc's gun. It was so quick that he became extremely frightened and begged Doc not to kill him.

Doc said, "Get on the next stage out of town, or you'll be hauled away in a box."

Johnny got on the stage. That was the last Doc saw of him until Doc's arrival in Leadville, Colorado, after his case at Pueblo had been dropped from the court's docket in 1882. There he met some of his old cronies from Tombstone.

"Doc, did you know your old friend Johnny Tyler is here?" asked one of them.

"That dirty son-a-bitch!" cried Doc. "Where?"

"Dealing at the casino. Hates your guts too for how you treated him back in Tombstone. Don't make no bones about it, either."

Johnny Tyler, still smarting from the humility heaped upon him by Doc, managed to talk Billy Allen, former chief of police and then acting as bartender at the Monarch Saloon, into a plan to embarrass Doc or get him killed. Allen had demanded the repayment of five dollars Doc had borrowed from him. He met Doc in Hyman's saloon, where Holliday fired at him almost on sight. The wound was not fatal, but Doc was arrested and jailed.

There was a lot of testimony given at the trial, both pro and con. The outcome was that Doc was acquitted and told to leave town permanently. I suppose Johnny Tyler was satisfied with that.

One day Wyatt and I were on our way for a drink, when we saw Doc standing in the road in front of a saloon, yelling vile words at Marshal Williams, a Wells Fargo agent. Williams was staggering drunk. There had been bad blood between these two for some time, and Williams had a gun in his hand.

Wyatt walked up to Williams and said, "Give me that gun," after telling Doc to cut it out.

Williams told Wyatt, "You'll have to take it."

So Wyatt grabbed the gun hand, and Williams pulled the trigger. The bullet went into a business place across the street, and Williams went to jail, but no one was injured.

As Wyatt started to lead Williams away, Doc said, "Wyatt, why the hell did you show up? I could have rid Tombstone of a no-good worthless bastard."

Williams later openly accused Doc of stage robbery, and Doc went hunting for him with blood in his eye, but Williams had departed.

One day Doc and John Ringo met on the street and got into an argument. Ringo challenged Doc to a fight and, had not Wyatt interfered, Doc would have killed him sure as hell. Johnny was drunk, and he couldn't have bested Doc even when sober. As Wyatt attempted to take Johnny to jail he jumped Wyatt, and Wyatt laid him low with a blow by his .45. Johnny never got over this and boasted that he would kill every Earp in Tombstone if he had to shoot them in the back.

Wyatt had a tough job. Half the citizenry was against him out of fear of the outlaws. The newspaper publisher John Clum blasted the fearful citizens and the outlaw element too. So did John Behan, whom Clum accused openly of being entirely too friendly with the outlaws.

One time Wyatt placed John Ringo in jail because he was suspected of being involved in a stage holdup. Then Doc and Wyatt rode to a ranch where the outlaws were holed up. To their great surprise, just as they reached the ranch, who should step out with a double-barrelled gun but Ringo.

He said, "I'm going to kill both of you S.O.B.'s."

Wyatt began trying to talk him down.

"John," he said to Ringo, "we know you can get one of us, but when you fire, the other will get you before you can shoot again. So think it over. You know it's the truth."

Ringo saw the logic of this, and, not being ready to die, he backed down and told them to ride off.

"And if either of you look back I'll blow you to hell."

Wyatt and Doc rode hurriedly back to town and found out that Behan had turned Ringo loose, without any authority, but with Ringo's promise to come to court at the right time. True to his word, Ringo made his appearance when his hearing was called. He was acquitted for lack of evidence. He laughed in Wyatt's face as he left the courtroom.

Wyatt was bucked all around. He busted many outlaws over the head and dragged them to jail when he had every right to kill them. And every one he arrested caused the outlaws to hate him all the more. One night I was gambling with Doc and Wyatt in a saloon when Ringo entered. He had been drunk for weeks and looked like a down-and-out buff hunter. He began cursing the Earps. Wyatt overlooked that. Then he attempted to pull a gun from his pocket. Wyatt jumped up and disarmed him, took him to the door, and shoved him outside.

When Wyatt returned to the game, Doc said, "Wyatt, you should have killed that bastard. He pulled a gun on you. He'd better never give me that chance."

Wyatt replied, "Doc, he was blind drunk. I can't see myself killing a drunken man. He'll be OK when he sobers."

Wyatt struck Ike Clanton so many times over the head and dragged him to jail that it's a wonder Ike knew how to walk.

One day Billy Clanton stepped in front of Wyatt on the street and said, "Wyatt, I am going to kill you. You have mistreated us Clantons for the last time. I have no fear of you or Doc either, or of your brothers."

Wyatt looked the young boy over and said, "Billy, you are only a boy, but a gun makes men equal. If you lay hand on that gun, I am going to put a bullet in your belly, just above that big belt buckle, and you know damn well I can do it."

Billy weakened. "Not now Wyatt — Doc's backin' you. But the time will come."

Wyatt slapped him hard across the face, lifted his gun from him, and carted him off to jail for packing a gun within the city proper.

The Benson stage was held up while it was carrying $80,000 in bullion. The outlaws did not get the bullion, but they killed the driver, Bud Philpot, and a passenger. Philpot was a rough old-timer who had been through many holdups. When the outlaws made their first move to stop the stage, Bud cracked his whip and yelled, "Get out of here!" He figured he might outrun them. Unfortunately, he did not.

Wyatt was a U.S. deputy marshal at this time, and he suspected Luther King, Larry Head, Bill Leonard, and Jim Crane of the Clanton outfit. He deputized his brothers Virgil and Morgan, Bat Masterson, Marshal Williams, and Doc

Holliday, and they headed for Drew's ranch, where these men had been seen nearby.

The posse ran down Luther King.

Behan said, "I'm against this. You have no charge against King."

Scared out of his wits, King said, "I only held the horses." But he named the other men who had been in on that particular holdup. He was turned over to Sheriff Behan, who was supposed to lock him up. Behan turned him loose instead, and King escaped into Old Mexico.

The other outlaws tried to tie Doc Holliday into the robbery.

Doc replied, "Had I pulled the robbery, I'd have gotten the money, and I'd have killed one of the stage horses."

Big Nose Kate got drunk and told Behan that Doc had been in on it. When she sobered up she changed her story. Doc ran her out of town, even gave her the money to leave on.

Wyatt made a deal with Ike Clanton whereby Ike would get the offered reward provided he gave Wyatt information leading him to the outlaws who were guilty, especially Head and Crane and

Leonard. Ike recruited Joe Hill and Frank and Tom McLaury to aid him. On the fourth of July Ike reported that these men were holed up in Eureka, New Mexico. He said he would try to get them to come to Rabbit Springs on the Bisbee Road, where Wyatt could surprise them.

The insidious trap was delayed while John Ringo, Jim Hughes, Old Man Clanton, Bill Johnson, Jake Gauze, and Charlie Snow raided a mule train in Skeleton Canyon that was carrying $75,000. Several figures were estimated as the number of the men killed while guarding the mule train, but I believe twenty would be close, perhaps more.

The outlaws celebrated for two weeks, and Behan, although he knew they had robbed the mule train, refused to bother them. Then Curly Bill, Milt Hicks, John Ringo, and others raided a herd of Mexican cattle, killing eight men. They drove the herd to the Clanton ranch and celebrated. When they were drunk, the Mexicans [from whom they had stolen the cattle] silently regained the herd. Later Curly Bill and his men overtook the herd, killed many more men, and brought the cattle back to the Clanton ranch.

Old Man Clanton knew he would be safe selling the cattle in Tombstone, so he set out for that town with the herd. On the way through Guadeloupe Canyon he and five of his cowboys were shot to death. Only one escaped — Harry Earnshaw.

There has always been a question as to who killed Old Man Clanton and his boys. I actually believe this was executed by Wyatt and Doc. Although they denied it, Earnshaw said he recognized their horses. Whoever did this job, it was great riddance of pure scum.

★ ★ ★

I would like to mention something here that has never been published that I am aware of. A man named Carter came to Tombstone from Texas — a real bad man, according to him. He joined up with Ringo and Curly Bill. He wasn't too well taken because he was a blowhard and the boys decided to sic him on to Doc. They figured whichever of the two

131

got killed it would be no great loss.

One day a scout reported that Doc had left town. Carter Stilwell, and Hughes waited for his return. They knew he wouldn't be gone long. When he returned they spread out across the road and blocked his way. He demanded to know what the hell was going on. Carter had his instructions, and he began throwing insults at Doc.

Doc realized they were out for a fight, so he told them, "The first man that reaches for a gun is going to die, and I'm not particular which one."

Hughes and Stilwell backed off and put up their hands, indicating they were not in on anything. Carter reached for his gun, and Doc shot him from his saddle. The other two set out for home grounds.

Doc figured the man was dead, and he rode back to the shack of a homesteader who had watched the whole affair from a distance. He gave the homesteader twenty-five dollars to bury Carter and told him to keep his mouth shut, which he agreed to do.

The homesteader later confided that he

dragged the man to his shack, and found that he wasn't dead. He couldn't bury a live man, so he dragged him into the shed to die. When his wife discovered the man was still alive, she began treating him. Slowly Carter recovered. He had money and paid them for this service. He hung around for a month, then left with the homesteader's sixteen-year-old daughter. Whether Doc ever learned that Carter had not been killed is doubtful.

★ ★ ★

After the stage robbery Joe Hill rode into Tombstone one day and reported that Jim Crane had died with Old Man Clanton. Wyatt urged Hill to keep after Leonard and Head, which he did. Hill later reported that he found them both dead. Those two bandits had been killed by the Haslett brothers, who ran a store in New Mexico. Wyatt sent his brothers, Virgil and Morgan, to investigate. They reported the story was true.

Some time later Ringo and Curly Bill rode to New Mexico and killed the two Haslett brothers in retaliation. A reward had been promised to the one reporting "dead or alive." It has never been found out who won it.

Wyatt received one reward, though. He had read a description of a man from Virginia City who was wanted for murder, and a $500 reward was advertised. One day on the street in Tombstone Wyatt saw the man, arrested him, and collected. This can be verified by Tombstone records.

One day a half dozen outlaws rode into Tombstone, and when they saw Morgan Earp alone and unarmed they told him, "If you ever try to arrest one of us we'll kill you."

It was common talk that the outlaws were out for the Earps and Doc Holliday. They made no bones about it, and the Earps continued to arrest them whenever the need arose.

On and on it went, and every arrest brought Earp closer to the O.K. Corral fight.

The O.K. Corral Fight

THE day before the O.K. Corral fight, on the 25th of October [1881], a hundred outlaws rode into town, roamed the streets, and raised hell in general. The Citizens Safety Committee wanted to appoint more men to aid Wyatt, but he thought it best not to. It might cause a general uprising. Then the committee made Wyatt, with his brothers, Virgil and Morgan, and Doc Holliday city marshals of Tombstone. This gave them more authority.

The morning of October 25th Ike Clanton was parading up and down the streets, carrying a rifle, yelling for the Earps to come out and fight. He ran into Virgil, and Virgil asked if he was looking for him. Ike came up with the rifle, and Virgil disarmed him, then banged him over the head with a .45 and dragged him off to jail.

About one o'clock on the afternoon of

the 26th Wyatt was informed that a gang had gathered at the O.K. Corral.

November 1st, 1881

I am purposely writing of the great fight which I witnessed in full at the O.K. Corral entrance between the Earp brothers, Doc Holliday, Billy Claiborne, Ike and Billy Clanton, Tom and Frank McLaury. Ike and Billy Claiborne ran out when the shooting started, proving what they have been suspected of by many, that they are cowards.

I have gone over every second of the fight in my mind, time and time again. I want my construction of this fight to be as accurate as possible. Some day I plan to write of my adventures in book form, and in the event my memory fails me in later years I can refer to this diary, which I keep in a ledger to have enough space to write as I wish.

November 3rd, 1881

Since my coming to Tombstone in 1879 the county of Cochise has been ruled by what amounts to a reign of terror. Outlaws are commonly referred to as cowboys. Not all cowboys are outlaws, but all outlaws are cowboys the way they herd stolen cattle over the desert. They ride the trails, robbing and killing travelers, robbing stages, and if they are arrested, they go free because people refuse to appear against them for fear of retaliation.

November 4th, 1881
Wyatt and his brothers Virgil and Morgan came to this town about a year ago to clean it up. I don't believe any lawman ever faced the odds that faced them. And I may say they have accomplished almost the impossible. They haven't killed anyone of note until the O.K. Corral fight, the 26th of October.

During their time they have arrested so many outlaws on minor crimes and caused them to pay so many fines that many of the outlaws have confined their activities elsewhere. They only come in to spend their ill-gotten gains. It's a wonder many of them can walk upright after being struck over the head with a pistol so many times. Tom McLaury wore a bandaged head into the O.K. Corral fight, put there by Wyatt when Tom gave some trouble. John Ringo is another victim, along with Tom and Frank McLaury and dozens of others. Every arrest adds to their hatred and to the insurrection at the Corral.

As can be noted, I am late in writing this, but with winter almost here I shall endeavor to catch up. Half the citizens and the sheriff's office favor the outlaws at every turn. John Clum at the newspaper rips them at every chance. He recently headed an article with this: "The sheriff of this county is entirely too friendly with the outlaws infesting this county."

Doc Holliday, a shady character from life's other side, came here with Wyatt, and he is a killer of note. I was in Santa Fe when he shot a man to death, then escaped from jail. Next I saw him here, an unpaid special officer allowed to pack a gun at all times. The outlaws and all others are required to place their guns in a designated place or pay a stiff fine. This has caused much hell-raising among the outlaw element, but Doc still wears his gun. He is a very little, consumptive man, who dresses immaculately at all times, more resembles a preacher than a professional gunfighter. He considers all men underlings and beneath his station in life, and he makes it stick, except for Wyatt, whom he favors.

The hearing for the Earps and Doc has been going on for some time. I expect to be called as a witness.

November 20th, 1881
I still have not been called to testify, and it looks now as though I won't be called. They are trying to prove that Tom Mclaury was not armed, and I can testify that he was, and after the fight Behan took Tom's gun, which has not been found. The hearing is over, and Doc and I were not called to testify. I have notified newspapermen that I will not make a statement for publication. I will write my version, and it will be kept in seclusion with access to no one until I see fit.

December 10th, 1881
This is my construction of the fight. It concurs with no newspaper account that

139

I have read or with any witness I have discussed it with.

About 1:30 P.M. on October 26th, 1881, I was busy at the stable when I saw Ike and Billy Clanton, Tom and Frank McLaury, later joined by Billy Claiborne, who wanted to be known as Billy the Kid. They all stopped near the entrance, talked, and drank from a bottle.

I sincerely believe that, had John Behan not come and talked to them, at least two of them would have left. It was their original intention. He delayed them several minutes with his talk, which I could not hear. I also believe, and I have discussed this with Wyatt, that he unwittingly caused the fight by having his pistol in his pocket instead of in a holster in plain sight. All of those men knew how swiftly Wyatt could bring a gun into action from a holster and I doubt very seriously that any of them would have tried him. This is only my conception.

Behan walked away after their talk, then came back quickly, and he said, "You men better scatter. The Earps and

Doc are on their way here."

The outlaws spread out and waited, Frank McLaury inside, Billy Clanton next — Billy and Ike Clanton; last in line was Tom McLaury; in back of Ike Clanton stood Billy Claiborne. Wyatt came in first with no pistol in sight and wearing a long black coat. Next came Virgil and Morgan Earp. They stopped in front of the outlaws.

One of them said, "You men are under arrest. Hand over your guns."

I fully believe they intended to submit to arrest. Slowly they drew their guns. They knew a fast move might invite disaster. Here they stood, four outlaws, each holding a gun. Tom at that time was not armed.

I refer to Doc Holliday as a lawman, although I don't think he fitted. All the lawmen were empty-handed, but Doc carried a shotgun. Frank McLaury surveyed the situation, as did the others. He noticed that Wyatt had no weapon in sight, and on the spur of the moment he decided to fight it out. He must have figured he would get Wyatt before he could reach his pistol in his pocket.

He jerked up his pistol and fired. About twelve feet separated them, and he missed. I knew Frank was a good shot, but facing a man like Wyatt unnerved him to the extent that he fired too quickly.

Before Frank could get off another shot Wyatt, unable to clear his weapon, fired through his coat. He didn't give Frank a chance to fire.

Frank buckled, dropped his gun, and fell almost at Wyatt's feet. I later saw that he had been struck in midsection. Then Billy Clanton fired at Wyatt and missed. He was trying desperately to reach the street. Wyatt told me later that when Billy fired he felt the ball pass his ear it was that close. By now Wyatt had his gun clear. He raised his arm, holding the gun at full length, and fired at Billy Clanton. He wanted him. When he fired, Billy staggered but did not go down. I saw later that Wyatt's bullet had struck under his arm. I saw Ike Clanton run behind Doc as Doc tried to bring his shotgun up. It folded in his coat, and Ike Clanton put on a burst of speed that a greyhound would have envied.

Doc said later "If that shotgun hadn't failed, I'd have killed that dirty bastard."

I saw Billy Claiborne run out, and when he passed Tom McLaury he handed Tom his gun. Tom had been struck and was on his knees in front of Doc. Tom jerked up the pistol and fired at Doc and just burnt his skin.

Doc brought up his shotgun and said, "I've been waiting for this chance for some time."

His first shot struck Tom in the midsection. Then Doc gave him the other barrel, and Tom fell over dead with a great hole in his belly. Doc threw down his shotgun, jerked out his revolver and fired point-blank at Billy Clanton. When Doc's bullet struck him, he fell to the street, then rolled over and died some time later. He had been struck several times.

Mr. Fly, the photographer became so excited that he ran and picked up Billy's pistol. As he stood up, Doc yelled for him to drop it or he'd put a bullet in him. Fly dropped the gun and ran inside his shop. The fight lasted but a few seconds. A taxi picked up Morgan and Virgil Earp and took them home. Both were wounded, but not seriously.

Doc and Wyatt reloaded quickly, fearful that the outlaws' friends might take up the fight. The sight of three dead or dying men in the street scared the others off. Curly Bill and Ringo were conspicuously absent.

Behan ran feebly in and informed Wyatt and Doc that they were under arrest.

Wyatt told him, "Get the hell out of the way."

What Doc said to him is unprintable. After a long hearing the court decided that they were within their rights as police officers. But the outlaws were not through by any means, and the people wondered when the next killing would take place.

The day after the fight the cowboys were buried, and the coroner's jury heard a parade of evidence. The pro-Earp *Epitaph* declared that the feeling among the citizens was that the officers were justified in their action. The town's other paper, in favor of the outlaws, did not agree; it said that the Earps and Doc were guilty of murder.

McLaury's brother who claimed to be a lawyer came to town to have the lawmen hung, he claimed. One day this brother met Doc on the street and began to quote the law to him.

Doc stopped him and said, "I just killed one of your brothers, and it wouldn't bother me one iota to pull the trigger on you too, you filthy bastard."

Whether this had any bearing on his leaving town is unknown.

The following is a letter addressing Judge Spicer immediately after the hearing; it appeared in the *Epitaph* with a comment by the editor that "On Saturday morning I received the following letter from the post office."

Tombstone, A.T. Dec, 13, 1881, to Wells Spicer.

Sir: If you take my advice you will take your departure for a more genial clime, as I don't think this one healthy for you much longer, as you are liable to get a hole through your coat at any moment. If sons of bitches such as you are allowed to dispense justice in this territory, the sooner you depart from us the better for yourself and the community at large. You may make light of this, but it is only a matter of time. You will get it sooner or later so with those few gentle hints I will conclude for the first and last time.

— A Miner

Judge Spicer's answer also appeared in the *Epitaph*:

I much regret that the writer of the above did not sign his name or at least inform me what mine he works in, for I could really be pleased to cultivate his acquaintance, as I think he would be an amiable companion — when sober.

As I cannot have the pleasure of a personal interview with this miner, will you allow me the privilege of replying to his charming epistle and say to him that I have concluded not to go, nor would I ever notice his disinterested advice on the subject

146

were it not for the fact that similar threats have been made by others and that the threats would be carried into execution if they only dared do it. Since the daring attempt to kill Mr. Clum and to wantonly kill a stage load of passengers to accomplish it, these little emanations of bravado do not draw forth admiration as would the beauty of summer clouds with silver lining. They are too sombre and surrounded with a black deathly shade of recent transactions.

They are bad omens of the future, when viewed in the light of the death glare of the past. This style of threat has been made not only against myself but at the same time against Mr. Clum and others. The attempt has been made to assassinate Mr Clum, the *Epitaph* Editor. Who will come next? One and all will ask from whence do these threats emanate. And each will have his own opinion. I have mine, and now I will try to do justice to the Clanton brothers by saying that they and men outside the city, living on ranches and engaged in raising cattle or other lawful pursuits, as heartily condemn the proceedings as any man in our midst, and that they as honestly denounce all such affairs as any man can, and that the real evil exists within the limits of this city.

It is needless to try to turn these matters into ridicule or to make them a subject of jest for funny quibs. It is a matter of serious importance to the community. I am well aware that all this hostility toward me is on account of my decision in the Earp case. For that decision I have been reviled and slandered beyond measure. Every vile epithet that a foul mouth could utter has been spoken of me, and principal among such being the charge of corruption and bribery.

It is but just to myself that I should here assert that neither directly or indirectly was I ever approached in the interest of the defendants, by them or for them. Not so the prosecution. In the interest of that side, even my friends have been interviewed with the hope of influencing me with money, and hence all this talk by them and those who echo their slanders about corruption. And here, too, I wish to publicly proclaim that everyone who says I was in any manner improperly influenced is a base and wilful liar.

There is a rabble in our city who would like to be thugs if they had the courage, would be proud to be called cowboys if people would give them that distinction. But as they can be neither they do the best they can to show how vile they are. They slander and abuse and threaten everybody they dare to. Of all such I say that, whenever they are denouncing me they are lying from a low, wicked, and villainous heart, and that, when they threaten me they do so because they are lowbred, arrant cowards and know that fight is not my racket. If it were they would not dare do it. In conclusion, I will say that I will be here just where they can find me should they want to.

— Wells Spicer

After the fight at the O.K. Corral livery stable, every known outlaw went on a rampage, swearing publicly that they would kill Earps and Holliday. Citizens wondered when the next killing would occur and it came on December 29, 1881. As the *Epitaph* printed their account:

About 11:30 last night, U.S. Deputy Marshal Virgil Earp was proceeding from the Oriental Saloon from the northeast corner of Allen and Fifth Streets to his room at the Cosmopolitan Hotel. When he reached the middle of the intersection, five shots rang out in rapid succession by unknown men who were standing in the old Palace Saloon that is being rebuilt next door above Trasker's and Pridham's store on the southwest corner of the same streets. Immediately after the firing the assassins ran rapidly down Fifth, past the combination shaft and disappeared in the darkness beyond Toughnut Street.

Two of the shots took effect on Mr. Earp, one badly shattering his left arm, and the other entered his left side.

How badly he is injured remains to be seen. Three of the shots entered the glass window of the Eagle Brewing Company. Immediately after the shooting three men ran past the icehouse, and the same three men were seen by a miner. After he was wounded, Virgil Earp walked into the Oriental Saloon and told Wyatt he had been shot.

Just after midnight on March 18, 1882, Morgan and Wyatt Earp were playing pool in Hatch's Pool Hall. Several shots were fired through a back window. One shot struck Morgan in the body, and he fell mortally wounded. Wyatt pulled his pistol and rushed into the alley. He found nothing but a drunk in a drygoods box, who had been awakened by the shots. He named the men who had fired the shots.

Wyatt called Doc and asked him to accompany the train with him to Tucson, carrying his dead brother and his wounded brother Virgil. In the Tucson yards Doc and Wyatt left the train to look for skulkers, fearful that they might try to finish off Virgil. Doc went into the depot, while Wyatt waited beside the train. He saw Ike Clanton run across the tracks, but he didn't have time to fire. Then Frank Stilwell ran across, and Wyatt killed him with a shotgun. He was found the next day by rail workers.

As soon as Behan found that one of his deputies had been killed by Doc and Wyatt, he immediately swore out warrants for them, but he never found the guts to serve the warrants. Wyatt and Doc were in the desert searching for Curly Bill and Pete Spence. Doc more especially wanted Ringo, along with the others. They found Indian Charley, and Wyatt killed him. He had been named as one of the killers.

When they had exhausted all efforts to find the outlaws, Wyatt and Doc returned to Tombstone and made preparations to leave town. They had had enough.

I fetched their horses to the hotel. They mounted in front of Behan and some of his outlaw friends. We all shook hands and wished each other luck, and they rode slowly down the street after Behan had suddenly remembered that he had warrants for their arrest.

Doc told him, "Don't try to serve them

unless you want a bullet in your head."

Several men rode along with Wyatt and Doc.

A Mexican boy had seen Wyatt killing Curly and Indian Charley. He lived near the springs. Wyatt had befriended this boy's family, so to return the favor the boy had ridden out and informed Wyatt that Curly Bill and his friends were at the springs. Wyatt and Doc told the others to hold up, and they went in on foot, figuring that too many would alert the outlaws. Hidden by sand ridges, they walked to within twenty feet of the outlaws, who were playing cards on a blanket.

Wyatt pulled back both hammers on his shotgun, then called to Curly Bill, who jumped for his rifle. When he raised up, Wyatt gave him both barrels. He fell, half cut in two. Those with him ran for the heavy underbrush, mounted, and rode off. Doc fired several shots at them as they fled, but the brush foiled his aim.

Pony Deal told me that he was with Bill that fateful day and saw him killed by Wyatt. They later returned and buried him at the spring. Doc was very put out over not having gotten Ringo, and he cursed his luck, as he later told Wyatt and Bat Masterson. (In 1920 Bat said that Doc was many terrible things, but he was not a liar.)

Bat said that after Tombstone Doc and Wyatt visited him at his gambling house in Trinidad, Colorado, and remained about two weeks, then left for Denver where Doc was immediately locked in jail. On the governor's desk were extradition papers from Arizona for Doc alone, charging him with the killing of Frank Stilwell. It looked for a time as though Doc would be returned to that state, but Bat and Wyatt secured an interview with the governor of Colorado and told the story — that Doc had taken no part in the actual killing, that Wyatt alone had killed Stilwell. After some consideration, the governor refused to honor the extradition, and Doc was freed.

Doc and Wyatt moved their lot to the gold fields west of Denver at Pueblo, but Doc left for about two weeks or so, and Wyatt had no idea where he was. Then Doc returned and told Wyatt this story:

Doc had an insane desire to kill Ringo, whom he hated with an uncontrollable passion. So he decided to return to the Tombstone area and kill him. He knew full well that if he was discovered in Arizona he would be hanged to the nearest tree or post, yet he took that chance. Getting killed didn't bother Doc to any great extent, for he had an incurable disease that would sooner or later claim his life anyway.

Outside of Tombstone he moved in with a family of Mexicans who owed him a debt of gratitude and who, he knew, would keep his secret. He watched the roads for some time, and whenever he saw Ringo, he was always in the company of too many others. Then one day fate favored him. Doe saw Buckskin Frank and Ringo dismount and sit beneath a tree to drink from a bottle. He didn't want to try them both, nor either one head on, for that matter. This might draw attention — not that he thought either could take him in a fight.

Soon he saw Buckskin Frank ride off, leaving Ringo alone. Ringo removed his boots and stretched out under a tree to sleep it off. Doc mounted and rode toward the sleeping man, surveying the area to make certain no one was about. When he reached the tree Ringo opened his eyes and said, "You dirty S.O.B.," and reached for his gun. Doc killed him. He sat and watched him expire, then rode back to the house to get his things and was soon on his way to Pueblo again.

Many people believed that Wyatt returned and killed Ringo, but Wyatt said he would never do anything that foolish. He said, "I wanted Ringo, but not that badly, but Doc was damn fool enough to try anything."

Note: No doubt the matter of Doc Holliday's statement that he killed John Ringo will cause a furor in many quarters. John Montgomery told it as it was told to him. It is felt that in such a controversial matter a bit of explanation should be given, as some will claim that Doc did not have the time to get to Arizona from Colorado because he was in a Pueblo jail.

The body of John Ringo was found on

July 13, 1882, in a clump of oak trees in Turkey Creek Canyon. It was believed he had committed suicide. Stuart Lake claimed that Johnny-Behind-the-Deuce O'Rourke killed Ringo; others said that Frank Leslie was the culprit. Since the coroner's verdict was listed as suicide, anyone who felt so inclined could have said that was so. According to the Minutes of the Common Council, Village of Tombstone, Wyatt Earp was listed as claiming the dubious honor.

Doc Holliday was arrested on a requisition from Arizona but Governor Pitkin of Colorado, on Friday, May 26, 1882, was urged not to honor it, since Doc would have no chance at justice in Arizona. He was arrested on a charge of swindling a man out of a hundred dollars for the sole purpose of keeping him in Colorado. On June 1, 1881, the *Pueblo Chieftain* reported that Doc Holliday appeared before Justice McBride on the swindle charge. He waived examination and was bound over to appear before the District Court. He was released on

$300 bond. It was another way to keep Doc in Colorado. The *Chief tain* reported on July 19,1882, that Doc Holliday was again in District Court on July 18, 1882, charged with larceny. Doc managed to keep himself under some Colorado indictment to prevent being extradited to Arizona. When the time was opportune, Doc left Colorado for other parts. Doc was also the kind of a man who might hightail it secretly back to Arizona to dispose of Johnny Ringo, some time between June 1 and July 18. One must remember that Doc was not confined to jail during that time.

Oddly enough, another factor appears on the scene. We have found mention of Doc in the Minutes of the District Court of Pueblo County, Colorado (Vol. 5, pp. 354 – 355), Case No, 1851, the People *vs* J.H. Holliday, for larceny, Court Appearance made on *July 11, 1882.*

If this is the case, Doc could not have been in Arizona when Ringo was killed. What puzzles us is the lapse of eight days before the *Pueblo Chieftain* reported this, as it did in its issue of July 19, 1882, especially since the news concerned such an infamous character as Doc Holliday. I suppose we'll never know. — W.M.

Doc Holliday — In Retrospect

DOC remained in the Denver area until he died at Glenwood Springs, Colorado, in 1886. Newspapers gave Wyatt credit for writing the following, though actually it was written by Bat Masterson. It appeared in the *San Francisco Weekly Examiner* in August 1886:

Doc was a doctor whom necessity had made a gambler a gentleman whom disease made a frontier vagabond, a philosopher whom life made a caustic wit, a long lean ash-blond fellow nearly dead with consumption and, at the same time, the most skillful gambler, and the nerviest, speediest, deadliest man with a six-gun that I ever knew.

John Henry Holliday, an aristocrat by birth, a professional man by education, a gunfighter and gambler by choice, had packed more violence and color into a brief lifetime than any other man of his wild age.

Bat Masterson and other participants in 1919 and 1920 told me this story, which has never been published. It proved that Doc did have some redeeming features.

One time, while Doc was visiting in Denver from the gold fields, he saw a young boy selling newspapers who was poorly clad and looked half-starved. Doc talked to the boy and asked about his circumstances. The boy told him that his mother had deserted him when he was a baby, and that he had been raised by an aunt who cared little for his welfare. He didn't attend school because he had to earn money for food.

Doc took a liking to the boy and promised to help him if he would go to school. He explained the importance of education. Then he made arrangements with a banker to give the boy money at a certain time every month. This continued for some time, and now and then Doc would visit the boy.

Bat did not know the boy's name,

but he knew a lady in Denver who might know it if I wanted the story. So when I was in Denver I called on this lady. Her name was Edna Burke. Her mother had operated a boarding house in Tombstone and had known Doc very well. She gave me the boy's name and told me the following story about Doc, which has never been published:

When Doc first arrived in Tombstone he engaged a room from Edna Burke's mother. He said he wouldn't take his meals with her but wanted a quiet place to sleep. They saw very little of Doc. Sometimes he would quietly come in and go to bed. Her mother had a young girl working for her, and this girl had a big young miner for a boy friend. One evening he came calling in a drunken condition, and the other roomers threw him out. This young man returned at about 3:00 A.M., stood in the street, and yelled for the roomers to come out and fight.

His yelling woke Doc, who slipped on his pants, poked a gun in his belt, and ran down to the street. He demanded to know what this young whelp meant by disturbing people at that hour.

The young man said, "Go on back to bed, for it's none of your business."

Doc replied, "I'm making it some of my business. You have a gun in your hand. Get to using it, and I'll put a hole between your eyes."

The young man tried to bring up his pistol, but he found himself looking down the barrel of Doc's cocked pistol. It scared him out of his wits. He dropped his gun and ran staggering down the street, and he never returned. The others in the house didn't know Doc then, but they were to find out a lot about him before he left town.

When Doc did leave Tombstone in 1882 he carried a trunk to Edna Burke's mother and asked her to keep it until he should write to tell her where to send it. Her mother subsequently left Tombstone herself, and because she had never heard from Doc regarding the disposition of the trunk, she took it along with her. Her mother later moved to Denver and when she read of Doc's death she opened the trunk for the first time. She found clothing, some small pieces of jewelry, and many letters from a girl named Mattie Holliday, who was Doc's cousin, as she found out. She read some of the letters. They were beautifully written, and there was no doubt that this girl was in love with Doc when she wrote them.

Edna Burke's mother wrote to this girl and asked if she would take the trunk and its contents. The girl replied that she would, and the letters and all were sent to her. In turn Mattie sent a gold cross and chain and explained that she could not carry on a correspondence because she was a nun.

Note: I have seen the cross and chain. The loss of the letters — for Mattie certainly destroyed them — is more than regrettable.

Had Edna Burke's mother only known how priceless they would be one day and kept them! Mattie was undoubtedly the one woman Doc Holliday ever truly loved, and she felt the same way about him. When he discovered he had an incurable disease, tuberculosis (in those days fatal), he must have told her that the best she could do was to forget him. Doctors had advised him to move to a dry climate for the possibly remaining two years he could expect to live.

Actually, Doc, despite his high living and gunslinging adventures, lived another sixteen years, and died peacefully in his bed. If only Mattie could have known! — W.M.

Edna Burke knew only part of the story of Doc and the boy he had sent to school. She didn't know the boy's name, but she knew where he had lived at that time, on a ranch north of Denver. It turned out to be large acreage with a beautiful house made of stone. The man was at first a little reluctant, but he invited me in. The first thing that struck my eye was a very large painting of Doc Holliday. After a few drinks he loosened up somewhat and said that the painting had been made from a picture of Doc that had been taken in Tombstone. He said that Doc had told him never to reveal their relationship, for being the adopted son of Doc Holliday would not help him any in life. As Doc Holliday lay ill he gave this young man a pistol, which now reposes under glass in the living room of the present family members.

He said, "I met Doc many times in Denver. He would take me here and there, but never to a saloon. Doc always resembled a Philadelphia lawyer the way he was dressed. I didn't know who Doc really was until years after he died. And the news I heard of him didn't alter my feelings for him, because Doc was the only person who ever helped me at all. I've never told people who come here and ask me about that picture. If I'd ever told them that I knew Doc personally they'd have laughed."

He told me that when Doc became desperately ill and was confined to a hospital at Glenwood Springs, he sent for 'the boy', who had by that time become a man.

"We talked for a long time, and Doc gave me a large check. He said he had no one else to give the money to. He told me a little about Mattie Holliday, his cousin, and he gave me a bundle of her letters that he told me to destroy. He said he didn't have the heart to do it himself. I didn't destroy them, because they were too beautiful to be thrown away. I'd never give permission to have one word of them published, for they are sacred to me."

So I bade this rancher farewell and left with a better feeling about Doc.

Years afterward I was in Denver again, and I called this man's house by phone. His daughter told me that he had been killed by a fall from a horse. She invited me out to the ranch, but she knew nothing about Doc's friendship with her father or very little. She said her father had attended college for two years on Doc's money and had majored in animal husbandry. She was in possession of some of Doc's letters, but would not give them up for publication. She let me see one of them, and the handwriting was magnificent, just as Mattie's handwriting had been.

In the parlor along with the painting of Doc and a Confederate flag, stood a giant, solid oak table. In the center was anchored a shatterproof glass dome which held the pistol Doc Holliday had given to Lee John White.

She said, "My father did not attend Doc's funeral, for he didn't know he had died until he read of it in the newspaper. But he visited his grave once a year as long as he lived."

She also told me the following story, which had not been mentioned by her father:

She said, "A Denver lawyer found out about the relationship between Doc and the boy that the bank was turning over money to every month. This lawyer decided to shake Doc for some money. So he faked a letter that was supposedly written by the boy's mother. At first Doc ignored the matter but then there came a formal letter informing Doc that unless he came up with a goodly sum for the boy's mother he would take Doc to court on a charge of non-support. He accused Doc of having fathered the child and deserting the mother. This was supposed to scare Doc. If he had been better acquainted with Doc, he'd have thought twice."

It seemed that Doc was living in

Creede, Colorado, at the time, and he invited the lawyer to visit him there. The lawyer bade farewell to his family and set out for a visit with Doc. He never returned. The family sent a detective to begin an investigation, so he called on Doc, who told him he had never seen the lawyer. This character kept poking around in the hope of finding out something.

One day Doc said to him, "You better get out of town. If you don't the buzzards will be fighting over your bones."

What became of the blackmailer has never been established. It was whispered that Doc took him for a ride to see the sights and left him in some deep canyon.

Doc did kill several men around Denver but he was accused of killing many more. A young city marshal, after Doc had killed a man, poked a gun in Doc's back and marched him out of town with instructions not to return. A few days later the marshal was found dead. Doc was accused but not held.

Another man struck Big Nose Kate, Doc's girl friend at the time he was in Tombstone and before. Doc hunted down this man, goaded him into a fight, and killed him.

And there is this last, close-at-home reminiscence of a schoolgirl during Doc's days in Tombstone [she was John Montgomery's daughter]:

She had strict instructions to avoid the main part of town on her way to school because of the wild men in the streets. Like most children, however her curiosity got the better of her now and then, and she would go to school right through town.

On one such day she met a fine-looking gentleman who asked her where she was bound. She told him to school, and that seemed to please him very much. He gave her a nickel, which in those days was great to a child. That man was Doc Holliday.

From then on she always walked through town, hoping to see him again. Frequently she did, and he never failed to give her a nickel, sometimes even a dime. He always told her how pretty she looked in her school clothes.

She also met Wyatt Earp many times,

but he only spoke and smiled. No nickel. She didn't take to him too well.

One day the teacher called on Wyatt to tell him about the grown boys who were riding around the school and yelling and carrying on for the benefit of the girls inside. She asked Wyatt to put a stop to it. He was so busy that he prevailed on Doc Holliday to scare the boys off.

Doc called at the school. Many of the boys knew of his reputation, and hurriedly left. He didn't threaten to shoot them. He merely asked them to leave and not return, since they were disturbing school activities. The teacher, a kindly soul, invited Doc to come inside. She was not aware of his reputation. He looked more like a preacher or a lawyer than anything else.

While in the school Doc gave a short lecture on morality and on the importance of getting an education. When the parents heard that this gunslinging gambler had talked to their children, they became highly disturbed. A number of them called on the teacher to reprimand her. They informed her that this sort of thing would not be tolerated — the very idea!

She told these callers to take their school and get themselves another teacher. This dimmed the picture considerably.

They pleaded in vain for her to return, and finally they called on Wyatt Earp. He said, "I doubt that I can be of any help. Perhaps you should call on Doc Holliday, for he seems to have a way with the ladies."

As a last resort they did approach Doc and ask for his help. Not for the parents, but because of his compassion for the children, he talked the teacher into returning. She promised to finish out the term.

Bat Masterson

WHO was this lawman, gun-fighter, Indian campaigner, Bat Masterson, whose name became synonymous with bold bravery and nerve many years ago? To what did he owe the fame that still lives on? Was it his personality? Or was it in the innovations he made in the methods he used as a lawman when he curbed crime and brutality in the streets of early-day small frontier towns?

Bat's attitude toward his name and place of birth remains an enigma. And why he picked the name of William Barclay, even signing it that way, over his baptismal name, has also never been explained. Bat never spoke of it, nor did members of his family, so far as is known.

Historians dug in old records for years for evidence that William Barclay Masterson, better known as Bat Masterson (whose life has been portrayed and publicized by Gene Barry on the television screen), was born in Iroquois County, Illinois, as he said he was. They came up against a blank wall. And small wonder.

Thomas and Catherine McGurk Masterson ran a farm near Lawrenceville, New York, close to the Canadian border. Shortly after their marriage they moved to Henryville, County Rouville, Quebec Province, Canada, about a hundred miles from Lawrenceville.

On September 22, 1852, their first child Edward J. Masterson, was born. Their next child would become famous, and for years his place of birth was debated back and forth. His baptismal record reads: "On November 27, 1853, Bartholomew, born yesterday to Thomas Masterson and Catherine McGurk, was baptized at this parish, County Rouville, Parish of St. George."

The County Rouville records indicate that the Masterson family lived there between the years of 1851 and 1855, and that Ed Masterson was also born there. The other Masterson children were born in Illinois. For reasons known only to himself, Bat Masterson changed his name to William Barclay and claimed that he had been born in Iroquois County, Illinois, near Fairfield.

Five more children followed: James P (1855 – 1895), Nellis (1857 – 1925), Thomas, Jr. (1858 – 1941), George (1860 – 1892), and Emma, known as Minnie (1862 – 1884). Like Jesse James's mother who favored Frank over her other children, Mrs. Masterson favored Ed over the rest of her brood. However, neither Bat nor the other children turned against their eldest brother because of this preference — Ed was too kind and gentle, too likable a person, engendering trust and faith in everyone he met. Even so, and in reverse, just as Frank James tried to protect Jesse, Bat did his best to keep trouble out of Ed's way.

Their father, Thomas Masterson, did not like Illinois, where he worked as a weightmaster for the Marshville Coal Company near Fairfield, so in 1867 the family moved to the vicinity of St. Louis, Missouri. There they homesteaded a section of land until May 1870, when they moved to Kansas and settled in Grant Township, Sedgwick County.

Along the frontier and in many small towns of that day education was almost nonexistent. Some children did get a primary education here and there, but it was largely hit-or-miss. Most education was self-taught or provided by a literate neighbor or friend. It is easy to understand why so many of the folks along the frontier could not read or write. So it was with the Masterson children.

Bat, like most young lads of the time, was more interested in firearms than in books. He had persuaded his father to get him an old pre-Civil war rifle, probably worth very little. Since wild game provided a large part of the diet of farm families of that day, guns were standard household equipment. Bat quickly mastered the use of the old Springfield, as well as the shotgun, and eventually became an expert as a pistol handler. In an age of deadly marksmanship with revolvers, he ranked among the best.

Sometimes the family would take the old spring wagon and ride into Wichita, Kansas, where Ed and Bat stared at the 'wonders' that met their eyes. The saloons, gambling dens, brothels, and other sights were things the boys had never seen before. The swaggering gunslingers and fancy dressed dudes made them gape in wonder. The boys decided then and there that they would have to see more of this.

In the Old West boys became men at an early age. So it was with Ed and Bat. They decided early on to go their own way and relieve their parents of being responsible for their welfare. They were anxious for adventure, especially for taking part in the buffalo hunting boom of that era.

Instead, they went to work for a grading contractor on the Atchison, Topeka, and Santa Fe Railroad, then coming through Kansas from the East. They worked long and hard at their backbreaking jobs, only to discover that their boss, a man named Raymond Ritter, had skipped out without paying them. Heartsick and missing his family, Ed decided to go home. Bat, on the other hand, was sure that Ritter would come back to Dodge City at one time or another. So he got a job with Tom Nixon driving a team and bided his time.

Ritter did return, of course. One day a friend of Bat's informed him that Ritter would be on the next day's train through Dodge. Early next morning Bat was at the train depot. Sure enough, Ritter alighted from the passenger car and strolled across the depot.

Ritter paled on seeing Bat, but kept on walking. Bat collared him and demanded the money owed him and his brother. Not much Ritter could do, seeing the mean look in Bat's eyes and the menacing .45 pistol held steadily in the hands of this teen-age boy. The onlookers cheered, none of them having much love for Ritter to start with.

Bat's manner in collecting their wages made a hit with most of the people in the area. Dodge City was then barely a town, merely the headquarters of the buffalo hunters who piled the buffalo hides in huge piles here and there.

Bat bought a Sharps rifle for a hundred dollars and decided to accompany buffalo hunters in the forbidden territory across the Arkansas River. Prior to 1870 few men had the nerve to venture south of

"Honest John" Montgomery (no relation to co-author Wayne Montgomery) once owner of the O.K. Corral, and one-time supervisor of Cochise County. Buried in Tombstone, Arizona, gravesite unknown.

Coyote Smith, who white men said was possessed of the devil, and the Indians called "Brother of the Evil Spirit."
(from photograph in Kansas State Prison file)

John Blane *(second from right, top row)*, a great-uncle of Wayne Montgomery, went West as a very young man. He and a companion were captured by Apaches and held captive for a year. Also pictured: other members of the Blane family. *(Wayne Montgomery)*

Doc (John Henry) Holliday, aristocrat, dentist, gunfighter and gambler. A deadly accurate shot, he was, on occasion, an officer of the law in company with his only close friend, Wyatt Earp. It was in that capacity that he took part in the O.K. Corral gunfight. *(Breihan Collection)*

Memorial Day parade, Tombstone, Arizona Territory, in the 1880s.
(Arizona Historical Society Library)

Allen Street in Tombstone, early 1880s. The O.K. Corral is located at the end of the structures on the right. *(Arizona Historical Society Library)*

Virgil Earp, who
assisted his brother
in his endeavors.

Wyatt Earp, legendary
law officer, who helped
rid such towns as
Dodge City and
Tombstone of outlaws.
His role in the O.K.
Corral shootout is a
matter of controversy
among historians. The
account of it by John
Montgomery in this
book is the first by a
direct eyewitness.

James Earp, *top* and Morgan Earp, *bottom*, who also worked with Wyatt as lawmen.

Ike Clanton, one of the outlaws involved in the O.K. Corral affair. He fled when the shooting started, but his brother Billy was one of the three fatalities.
(Arizona Historical Society Library)

The only verified photo of John Ringo, friend when sober, fiend when drunk, which was most of the time. He cast his lot with Tombstone's outlaws.
(Courtesy of John Burrows)

Buckskin Frank Leslie, whose speed and accuracy with the six-gun was the equal of any gunslinger of the day. He stalked the streets of Tombstone wearing a Prince Albert coat, with a revolver attached to his belt by an engraved silver clip.

Front Street in Dodge City, crossroads of the Frontier, universally recognized as Queen of the Cowtowns, and in its heyday reputed to be the "wickedest city in the West."

(Kansas State Historical Society)

The popular and dapper William B. "Bat" Masterson. As an assistant marshall under Wyatt Earp, he patrolled Front Street carrying a silver-headed walking stick, which he used to crack the heads of trouble-hunting wildmen – hence the name "Bat." For a time sheriff of Dodge City, later moving on to Tombstone, he was a longtime friend of John Montgomery. *(Kansas State Historical Society)*

Chavez's Hole after the fire at the Ludlow Tent Colony. *(Colorado Historical Society)*

Procession of coal miners alongside hearses carrying the 21 victims of the Ludlow Massacre down the streets of Trinidad, Colorado.
(United Mine Workers of America)

Prof. Miss KATIE BENDER

Can heal all sorts of Diseases; can cure Blindness, Fits, Deafness and all such diseases, also Deaf and Dumbness.

Residence, 14 miles East of Independence, on the road from Independence to Osage Mission one and one half miles South East of Norahead Station.

KATIE BENDER.

June 18, 1872.

Announcement of "Kate Bender's" presumed gifts by which she enticed the unwary to their doom. *(Kansas State Historical Society)*

The house Kate Bender built near Independence, Kansas, where she killed and robbed many unsuspecting wayfarers. The graves in which she buried the corpses were subsequently exhumed, but by then "Kate" was safely far away. Before her death, she made a confession to the minister of the Protestant church she then faithfully attended.

Lige Redstone, the courageous, lovingly respected cattleman who imparted to a young man he hired (Wayne Montgomery) much of his wisdom and the moving story of how he took his family West.

the Arkansas, as it was almost certain death to do so because of the buffalo. But by 1874 the herds had been practically exterminated in Kansas. Bat had one close call with a half-dozen braves from the tribe of Bear Shield. They robbed him of his horse, guns, and inflicted a blow to his forehead, cutting it severely. He stumbled back to camp and asked his companions to assist him in retrieving his property. He got no takers. The men were anxious now to head for Dodge City and safety. Bat, however was not to be denied. During the night he located the Cheyenne camp and ran off a number of horses, which he sold in Dodge at a good price.

Although the government had negotiated a treaty with the Indian tribes, the disputed territory where the buffalo now migrated lay in the state of Texas. When Texas was readmitted to the Union in 1870 after having seceded during the Civil War it retained all its public lands. it wanted Indians out of these areas. Since it had not been consulted in the matter Texas paid no heed to the treaty and made no efforts to enforce it.

Following the Treaty of Medicine Lodge, the government sent troops to patrol the Arkansas, no easy matter for buffalo hunters wishing to cross into the forbidden territory. The buffalo hunters and the Indians were natural enemies. They hated each other as much as an honest rancher hates the rustler. The buffalo was to the Indian what cattle were to white men, and more. The bison provided them with food and hides for their tepees, as well as tools, toys, grease, and literally all the staples of their life.

In the spring of 1874, A.C. Myers led a party from Dodge City into the disputed territory. The party consisted of a hundred men and wagons; their destination was the territory near old Adobe Walls. The Myers train crossed the Arkansas River at Dodge and made Crook Creek at sundown. The noted frontier scout, Billy Dixon, was one of the party. James Hanrahan, a saloonkeeper was another; Bermuda Carlisle, a scout and buffalo hunter was also among the men, as was Dutch Henry Born. Last, but not least, the youngest one was Bat Masterson. In later years Bat became sheriff of Ford County. In that office he was to arrest the infamous Dutch Henry, charged with horse theft.

Jim Hanrahan used sod in constructing his saloon.

O'Keefe threw up a shack for use as a blacksmith shop.

Another sod house was erected to house the Rath & Wright Store. Rumors reached them that the Comanches and Kiowas were on the war path on account of the invasion of Texas territory by the buffalo hunters.

There were twenty-eight men and one woman still at the camp at Adobe Walls on June 27, 1874, when Chief Quana Parker of the Comanches and his allies swept down upon the settlement. Just prior to the attack a phenomenon occurred that has never been explained to this day. Mike Welch and bartender Shepherd had retired to their bunks, and all lights were out. Suddenly a sharp cracking sound rent the still air. Both men leaped from their bunks.

"It's the ridge pole!" called Welch. "Too much weight on the roof. Got to prop it up."

Bat Masterson took a look at the pole and said, "Welch, you must have been dreaming. That pole is as solid as your head."

Then a bugle sound blew 'Charge', and soon the Indians were coming full speed toward the buildings. Billy Dixon darted for Hanrahan's place, shouting warnings on the way.

Above the buildings, to the north, a picket corral had been built. There the Shadler brothers and their dog were killed in their wagon in the first charge. Sheltered in Rath & Wright's Store building were manager James Langton, George Eddy, Billy and Mrs. Olds, Tom O'Keefe, Andy Johnson, and Sam Smith. In the Myers and Leonard Store were old man Keeler, Harry Armatage, Ed Trevor, Frank Brown, Jim Campbell, Billy Tyler, Dutch Henry Born, 'Frenchy', Mike McCabe, 'Fred Leonard', and Henry Lease. Hanrahan's saloon was defended by Billy Dixon, Billy Ogg, Hiram Watson, Bermuda Carlisle, Jim Hanrahan, James McKinley, bartender Shepherd, Mike Welch, and Bat Masterson.

Time and time again the Indians, riding

in pairs, braved the hail of lead in order to pick up their fallen companions who lay either dead or wounded before the buildings. Dixon and Masterson stood shoulder to shoulder at a window and made every shot count. The Indian bugler a renegade white, was killed while trying to loot the Shadler wagon. Billy Tyler and Fred Leonard, during a lull in the fighting, slipped outside and into the stockade to get a better shot at the Indians. They were discovered, and the Indians wounded Billy Tyler; he died within the hour. Leonard managed to escape to safety.

On the third day the Indians were congregated on a high bluff across the valley. Billy Dixon took his .50-caliber rifle, aimed it, and let the hammer fall. One of the Indians dove headlong from his pony's back. Later the distance was measured off and found to be 1,538 yards, indeed a remarkable shot. This discouraged further attack by the Indians.

After Adobe Walls Bat and Billy Dixon returned to Dodge City. Because all buffalo hunting had been stopped by the Indian war both young men signed up with Colonel Nelson A. Miles to act as scouts. They were to work out of Fort Dodge under the direct command of Lieutenant Baldwin, who had been ordered to the area of the Staked Plains in the Texas Panhandle. During that time the column was attacked by a large force of Indians and pinned down until the arrival of reinforcement with a Gatling gun. The Indians broke, pursued by the cavalrymen.

While on a scout in November Bat discovered a large Indian village on McClellan Creek. The charge was such a complete surprise that the Indians fled as fast as they could.

The attack resulted in the safe recovery of two Germain sisters, whose parents had been killed by the Indians in another raid.

After the Indian campaigns, Bat went back to Dodge City in the summer of 1876, suffering from a pelvis wound that would bother him the rest of his life. It was about this time that Bat discarded his prairie garb and began to wear suits, vests, starched shirts, and all. At first he wore flashy guns, one a silver-plated

Colt Peacemaker with a 7½″ barrel. The grips were pearl-carved with an eagle, and the backstrap was engraved, "W.B. Masterson." Through the years the Colt Arms Company made seven more pistols for Bat, all nickel-plated, with shorter barrels. He also owned a Buntline Special, which the lurid fiction writer Ned Buntline, presented to him, but it was so long that it is doubtful Bat carried it often.

The political marshal of Dodge City was a man named Larry Deger who cared little about enforcing the law, leaving that chore to his assistant, Wyatt Earp (later of O.K. Corral fame). Earp was well acquainted with the past actions of Bat, and offered him a job as a police officer. Bat hated the job of being a local peace officer. It was too conflicting, and the work connected with it seldom needed quick wit or fast gunplay. His chief duties were to keep the peace among the Texans who drove their cattle to Dodge City, and do so with tact and goodwill in order not to offend the men who were bringing big money into the town. At that time he was still suffering from his wound. When patrolling Front Street he carried a walking stick for several weeks and used it to crack the heads of several wild men hunting trouble. Thus the nickname 'Bat'.

In 1877 we find Bat a long way from Dodge City. He had resigned his policeman post and was traveling through other western towns, gambling most of the time, a sport he found invigorating and one that needed skill and bluff to win. He had decided to visit Deadwood, South Dakota. Realizing, however that most gold claims would have already been staked, he went to Nebraska in search of adventure. There he again ran into Wyatt Earp. Earp told Bat he had just been offered the job of marshal at Dodge City. Would Bat be interested in being his chief deputy?

Bat was not interested, but he did accompany Earp to Dodge, his thought being to earn more money over the gaming tables than trying to keep the peace for little or nothing. A run-in with the now deposed ex-marshal, Larry Deger made Bat change his mind about being a peace officer. Bat had tried to stop a fight when Deger and some of his cohorts pistol-whipped him and threw him in jail. Boiling with indignation and nursing a lacerated scalp, Bat was easily convinced by the Republicans to run for sheriff of Ford County.

It would not be a cinch, as Deger had also filed for the office of sheriff. Deger had a lot of politicians, trail drivers, and cattle barons on his side, and Bat had the backing of the respectable storekeepers and most of the citizens and others who wanted Dodge City kept peaceful. The wily Bat also bought an interest in the Lone Star Dance Hall to cover his backside should the election be won by Deger.

It was close. Bat ran on this platform: "While earnestly seeking the sufferages of the people, I have no pledges to make, since most such are not kept after an election anyhow."

To emphasize this, the *Dodge City Times* wrote: "He knows how to gather in the sinners, is qualified to fill the office, and, if elected, will never shrink from danger."

All this worked well for Bat. It appeared

that his popularity won over the political influence of Deger. The election of November 1877 put Bat Masterson in the sheriff's seat by three votes!

One of Bat's first encounters with a major outlaw happened just after the robbery of the Santa Fe train at Kinsley, Kansas. The railroad and Wells Fargo Express demanded action. They sent Detective Hudgens to seek Masterson's help. Bat told the officer that the robbery had occurred in Edwards County and not in Ford County, which was out of his jurisdiction. However he agreed to help. In some manner Dave Rudabaugh, leader of the robbers, was induced to come into Ford County. Bat arrested him at once and demanded to know where he got all the money he was carrying. Dave Rudabaugh, backed into a corner was never without a way to slip out through the back door. He agreed to betray his men if granted immediate freedom.

Whatever glory is given to Masterson and Hudgen for rounding up the Rudabaugh gang during a violent snowstorm as the men huddled around a fire at Lowell's cattle camp, it was Rudabaugh who made the capture possible. These were not the kind of men to be taken by surprise even in a raging blizzard. Not a shot was exchanged. The men were trapped before they realized that their own leader had betrayed them.

Rudabaugh went on with his life of crime. His second last escape occurred in Las Vegas, New Mexico. He had been tried in Santa Fe on February 16 for robbing a train and a stagecoach. He pleaded guilty and was sentenced to twenty years on each count. Meanwhile the authorities in Las Vegas insisted that he be brought there to stand trial for murder. They won out. As the wagon left Santa Fe, Judge Prince said of Rudabaugh, "That man will never hang."

Rudabaugh languished in the Las Vegas jail from February 27 to December 3, 1881. He was not without outside friends. A case knife and a pick without a handle were smuggled in to him. Ten men were in the cell with him, and all were in favor of escape. Those not chained took turns in picking at the cement, the debris dropping noiselessly on the mattresses.

Never once did the four guards who slept across the plaza from the cells realize what was going on. The escape was a success. It was not discovered until feeding time at seven o'clock the following morning.

Since Dave Rudabaugh was the only prisoner wearing leg irons, he lagged behind the others. At Naranjo, six miles above Las Vegas, he found someone to cut his chains. He returned to Arizona, where he resumed his life of robbing and cattle rustling, was finally caught, again escaped from the jail at Tombstone and went to Mexico. His exit from this earthly life occurred at Parral after he had committed several robberies there. A man in a mob that charged Dave brandished a sword and severed his head from his body and stuck it on a pole. The *Las Vegas Optic* in its issue of February 23, 1886, gives a graphic account of Rudabaugh's death.

Some biographers have given Wyatt Earp credit for the capture of Dave Rudabaugh in Kansas. Not so, although Earp did trail Dave for robbing the mails. Fifty years after the event Earp said of Rudabaugh: "Rudabaugh was about the most notorious outlaw in the range country. He was a rustler and robber by trade with the added specialty of killing jailors in the breaks for liberty at which he was invariably successful whenever he was arrested. After a series of holdups, word came that Rudabaugh and Roake were in Texas, and, as I was a deputy U.S. marshal, I was offered ten dollars a day and expenses to get them."

Things were going well for Bat back in Dodge City, but when his brother Ed came to town in December 1877, it scared Bat half to death. Even more so when Ed decided to sign on as a deputy marshal of Dodge. Bat feared that Ed's docile nature and trusting ways would get him into trouble. And it did. Four months later, on April 9, 1878, Ed came upon a crowd of noisy Texans as he was making his usual rounds. These men were armed, so Ed took a gun away from a man named Jack Wagner and handed it to one of the other men; then turned and walked away. Wagner pulling another gun from his pocket, shot Ed in the stomach. Ed Masterson managed to draw his own revolver and fire several shots amid other shots being fired as well. When the smoke cleared, Ed Masterson, Jack Wagner and Alfred Walker lay writhing in the street. Bat came rushing upon the scene. Ed had staggered into a saloon, where he collapsed. Bat took him to his own room. As Ed lay dying in his arms, Bat wept like a baby. Ed was buried at Ford Dodge.

Many writers have stated that Bat killed Wagner and Walker to avenge Ed's murder. Not so. Wagner died the next morning as a result of the wound received during the shooting. He was buried April 11, 1878, on Boot Hill. Nearly two months later on June 1, 1878, the *Dodge City Times* reported, "Alfred Walker who has been confined to his bed ever since the unfortunate scrape last April, was removed to Kansas City last Friday where he is still under medical treatment."

Charlie Bassett was appointed city marshal of Dodge City to replace Ed Masterson, with Wyatt Earp named as his assistant. And, apparently, the death of his older brother did not deter the decision of Jim Masterson to become a deputy marshal of Dodge City.

Early in July the comedian team of Eddie Foy and Jim Thompson appeared at the Brown & Springer Comique Theater to put on a show for Dodge City. An incident occurred there at that time that made Bat and Foy friends for life. Foy gives this account of it in his book, *Clowning Through Life*:

There was only one time that I was ever shot at, though I've been threatened often enough. Ben Thompson, the Texas scrapper, gave me an opportunity one evening to increase my reputation for courage — with others, I mean; not with myself. Thompson was not highly popular in Dodge, Bat Masterson being one of his few friends. Thompson, about two-thirds drunk, blundered in back of the scenes at our place one evening between acts; . . . Seeing me, he drew his gun and called out, "Getcher head outa the way, I wanta shoot out the light."

The light was an oil lamp on the table at my elbow, and on the other side of me from him. Thompson didn't like me, possibly because he knew I didn't like him. Now I was fooled with this foolish obstinacy. I wasn't going to move my head just because a drunken bum like Thompson wanted to shoot out a lamp. Neither was I going to let him think that he could scare me. So, although I had turned my head to look at him, I didn't lean back, but just sat with my eyes fixed on him as imprudently as I could.

"Getcher head outa the way, I told you," he yelled. "I'm gointa shoot out that light. if you want it through yer head, too, all right!"

With that he pointed his gun full at me, while I sat staring full at him, hypnotized by my own stubborness.

For a long time we confronted each other — and then Bat Masterson burst into the scene, threw the muzzle of Thompson's gun upward, and partly by coaxing and partly by shoving got him out. When they had gone, I found my hand shaking so that I couldn't put on any makeup. I was limp for the rest of the evening.

Business in Dodge was good and Bat took all of it in his stride. Booming cattle business and the many saloons and brothels brought loads of money into Dodge City, and it prospered. Bat was also busy with his law enforcement. At one point he captured a man named Davis, who was a fugitive from Fort Lyons. A few days later Bat wounded a man named George Hoy when he and Earp fired upon a bunch of cowboys who had been shooting up the town and had turned to flee. Hoy died sometime later of complications that set in after the injured leg was amputated.

No doubt the actions of Bat were condoned by the people of Dodge and by the press, for on August 16, 1878, the *Dodge City Times* paid Masterson and his deputies the following praise:

Sheriff W.B. Masterson and Deputy William Duffy are indefatigable in their efforts to ferret out and arrest persons charged with crimes. Scarcely a day passes without reward for their vigilance and promptness. We do not record all these happenings because evil doing is of such common occurrence. There is a pleasant contemplation in the fact that we have officers who are determined to rid the community of a horde that is a blight upon the well being of this overridden section.

The legend that Clay Allison treed Dodge City and caused all officers to seek shelter is pure nonsense; no substantiation can be found to verify it. It appears that Bat was selected as the 'goat' to bear the brunt of this supposed affair even if it did happen. Range Detective Charlie Siringo stated it occurred on a day in October 1878.

The death in early October 1878 of Dora Hand, an actress in Dodge, was a real tragedy, more so because she was shot and killed by James Kennedy by mistake. During a time when Mayor 'Hound-dog' James Kelley was ill and away from home, Dora Hand asked permission to use his house. It was granted. Kennedy had vowed to kill Kelley over some dispute and laid his plans to do so, not knowing that the mayor no longer occupied the home.

James Kennedy, knowing the location of Kelley's bed, fired two shots through the door killing Dora Hand as she slept. Without checking to learn the result of his deed, Kennedy rode his horse out of town. That afternoon Sheriff Masterson, Deputy Duffy, Charlie Bassett, and Wyatt Earp followed Kennedy's trail to Meade, Kansas. Kennedy was later tried before Judge Cook and acquitted.

While Bat Masterson had taken on the cloak of the law, his Adobe Walls fight friend, Dutch Henry Born, had taken to the rustling trail, stealing horses from ranches, as well as from government forts — Fort Dodge, Fort Elliott and others. Dutch Henry had a well-established ring of horse theft bases all through that part of the country. He did so well that the cavalry and posses were after him and his gang most of the time. The only person to escape Henry's art of rustling was Charles Goodnight, whose ranch was in the Texas Palo Duro Canyon. He made a pact with Dutch Henry in order that his horses would not be molested.

Finally, a detachment of cavalry from Fort Elliott, under the command of

Captain Wirt Davis, ran into a contingent of the band of horse thieves. In the ensuing battle Captain Davis was wounded in the abdomen and two of the six outlaws killed. So incensed were the soldiers at the death of their captain that they took the remaining outlaws and hanged them from the cottonwood trees along the river bank.

Dutch Henry was in the Indian Territory at the time of this incident with one of his lieutenants named John Terry. On hearing of the fate of some of his men, Henry rushed to Colorado, swearing he would never steal another horse. His freedom was short-lived, however for he was arrested in Trinidad. The *Daily Rocky Mountain News* at Denver said this under date of January 3, 1879: "Dutch Henry, the notorious thief of Kansas, Indian Territory and Texas, was arrested here last night by Sheriff Wooten. The sheriff from Dodge City, Ks., is here after him."

Sheriff Bat Masterson left with his prisoner for Dodge City on January 5, 1879, where Dutch Henry was to stand trial for horse stealing. Apparently the whole thing seemed a farce to some people. The Trinidad Enterprise, in its issue of January 5, 1879, seemed to think so:

Considerable merriment was created in Justice Walkers court on Saturday, during the hearing of Dutch Henry's case, by Sheriff Masterson of Dodge City, Kansas, insinuating that the attorney for the defense, Mr. Salisbury, had left Kansas under a cloud.

Dutch Henry had left Colorado and returned to Kansas. He agreed to waive his rights and to save trouble and delay of having a requisition made upon the governor of Kansas. Accordingly, he went east with Sheriff Masterson on Sunday morning. Of course, he was not ironed, and was not really a prisoner.

Bat and his prisoner arrived in Dodge City amid cheers and congratulations from his loyal constituents. However, all was in vain, for Dutch Henry Born was acquitted.

In March 1879, Dutch Henry was

rearrested in Trinidad on an old charge pending from his escape from jail in Arkansas. After his release he went to Creede, Colorado, later marrying Ida Dillabaugh, a native of Montague, Michigan. After their marriage on July 10, 1900, Dutch Henry and his wife filed a claim on lake property high in the mountains on the West Fork of the San Juan River in Mineral County, Colorado. Dutch Henry Born, King of the Horse Thieves, died on January 10, 1921, at Pagosa Springs, Colorado. To this day the lake on the property is called Born Lake.

On January 18, 1879, Bat Masterson was appointed a United States deputy marshal, giving him authority in every state. During the months of March and June of that year in his new peace officer capacity, Bat and his men quelled possible riots between two rival railroads, the Denver & Rio Grande and the Atchison, Topeka, and Santa Fe. Each company was accusing the other of lease violations, but in the end, all was settled without a shot being fired.

Little by little, Bat's fearsome reputation

had been growing. People thought he would have no problem winning the election, which was close at hand. On October 25, 1879, the *Dodge City Times* said this:

W.B. Masterson, the nominee for the office of sheriff;

Bat is acknowledged to be the best sheriff in Kansas. He is the most successful officer in the state. He is immensely popular and is generally well liked. Horse thieves have a terror at the name of Masterson. He was the unanimous choice of the Independent Convention, and will be elected by a heavy majority. Every hater of horse thieves will rejoice over Bat's triumphant election; and friends of good order and peace will contribute to his success.

Of course, as in any election, vicious rumors began to be spread about Bat's honesty, claiming he demanded payment for services rendered from time to time. Also, some people thought he was spending too much Ford County tax money in rounding up outlaws and horse thieves in other counties, as well as in his own.

The Peoples' Ticket had nominated George Hinkle to oppose Masterson for the office of Sheriff of Ford County, Kansas. Although the general consensus was that Bat would win in a landslide, it did not turn out that way He lost to Hinkle by a vote of 268 to 404. The Dodge City Times published the following on November 8, 1879: "There is a good deal of speculation as to the cause of the late defeat in Ford County of the Independent Ticket. We conjecture the most powerful influence was in the beer keg; of course, the people fighting for reform and honesty wouldn't use money." On January 12, 1880, George T. Hinkle was sworn in as sheriff of Ford County, Kansas.

Thoroughly disgusted with politics, Bat left Dodge City and traveled farther west. He was in Leadville, Colorado, in February 1880, suddenly finding himself interested in the business end of things there. Gunnison County was on the move, he told Charlie Bassett and others, and if they were wise they would invest money there.

He returned to Dodge City to participate in the Ford County Republican Convention as a delegate. In May 1880 he learned that the Gunnison County venture had been a slick fraud, and he warned his friends to refrain from investing any money in supposed mines in Pitkin or Gunnison counties.

In June Bat heard from his friend Ben Thompson, who asked for Bat's help in getting his brother Billy out of Ogallala, Nebraska, where he had been wounded in a gunfight. Bat and Ben were good friends, although there was little love lost between Bat and Billy Thompson. On arriving in Ogallala, and since Ben Thompson had been barred from coming into Nebraska, Bat and some friends staged a mock fight in a local bar. During the confusion Bat was able to whisk Billy Thompson from his hotel room and carry him to a waiting railroad sleeping car. He took the wounded Billy to Buffalo Bill's ranch on the North Platte, where he recovered in due time.

He spent some time in Tombstone,

Arizona, a good deal of that time dealing faro in the Orient Saloon. One time he also acted as a deputy in one of the posses formed by Wyatt Earp. Bat was in New Mexico when a message arrived from his brother Jim, then ex-marshal of Dodge City, asking for his help in clearing up a dangerous matter that had cropped up. The whole trouble had started when Jim Masterson and A.I. Peacock disagreed about whether or not Al Updegraph, one of their bartenders in a saloon owned jointly by Masterson and Peacock, should be fired. Jim demanded the dismissal of Al, while Peacock disagreed with that decision. Things became so bad that in their anger both men fired at each other with consequences.

On Saturday, April 16, 1881, Bat arrived in Dodge City and immediately looked for his brother. As he walked along the grade that ran along the railroad tracks, he sighted Updegraph and Peacock coming across the street. Both men went for their guns as they saw Bat. Bat took refuge behind the grade embankment; Peacock and Updegraph ran for the safety of the jail building.

Bullets began to fly from every direction. It seems that others wanted to get into the fight too. During the fight Updegraph was wounded in the chest, not fatally. It was never really ascertained whose bullet had hit Updegraph, one of Bat's or one fired by the others who had joined in the fight.

During a lull in the firing, which had lasted about ten minutes, Mayor A.B. Webster strolled into the plaza, stating he would use his shotgun on anyone who began firing again. He and Marshal Fred Singer escorted Bat off to the jailhouse, charged with disturbing the peace. In lieu of arrest, others involved in the ruckus were asked to leave Dodge City. Bat was fined the modest sum of eight dollars for disturbing the peace and dignity of the town.

It had been an unfortunate affair. The indiscriminate firing of weapons had endangered innocent lives, as well having done considerable damage to the buildings in the vicinity. Soon afterward Bat managed to have the partnership between Jim Masterson and Peacock ended; he then took Jim with him to New Mexico. Bat then traveled to Trinidad, Colorado, where he operated a gambling hall in one of the larger saloons in that city.

By this time events in which Bat had participated gave him the name of 'Killer Bat' by some. Of course, Bat resented this undue label and also the short item that appeared in the *Ford County Globe* on February 25, 1883: "The Times of Dodge City says that Jack Bridges has been city marshal of that town. Jack, like Wild Bill and Bat Masterson, belongs to the killer class and it is only a question of time when he will lay down with his boots on."

In response to this Bat said, "I have no desire to return to the delectable burg, as I have long since bequeathed my interest in Dodge City and Ford County to the few vampires and murdering band of stragglers who have controlled its political and moral machinery in the last few years."

Oddly enough, Bat did return to Dodge City in June 1883, this time to assist his old friend Luke Short, the gambler who had slain Big Jim Courtright, noted gunfighter and strikebreaker. Although Dodge had passed an ordinance prohibiting gambling within the city limits, the law was not being enforced for all concerned. Mike Sutton, prosecuting attorney, played favorites when it came to this matter, Luke Short not being one of those favored. So Luke called for Dave Mathers, Bat Masterson, and Wyatt Earp to come to his aid. The call was answered.

Colonel Thomas Moonlight, the adjutant-general of Kansas, was named chairman of a peace commission to settle the matter once and for all. Apparently Mike Sutton did not appear at the meetings, since the newspapers reported he had gone to his tornado cellar until after the truce was over. As it was, Luke got what he wanted, and all other gamblers got a fair shake as well. The June 5, 1883, issue of the *Ford County Globe* printed this: "The gambling gentry smile and are happy again, since they are allowed to spread their layouts again."

Bat went from pillar to post, trying to find a spot that would suit him as a permanent place to settle down. He went back and forth from Trinidad to Dodge City many times, usually during an election time, seeing that his friends got a fair deal at the polls. In March 1886 Bat returned to Dodge and made a general cleanup of the town, closing the saloons and chasing the gamblers out of town. From that project he went to Denver, Colorado, and started in business as a gambler and operator of a burlesque theater.

Bat operated his place in an honest manner. It was not long, therefore, before the local police began to harass him. One night two officers came into his place, intending to arrest him on some trumped-up charge. Bat ran them from the building. The chief of police soon barged into the saloon, threatening Bat for intimidating his men. Bat politely grabbed the sputtering chief by the nose and escorted him from the building.

"Now, damn you, stop bothering honest gamblers!" Bat told the astonished and embarrassed chief of police.

We next find Bat the operator of the Palace Theatre in Denver. There he met Emma Walters, a blonde song-and-dance girl, whose home was in Philadelphia. It was a short romance. On November 21, 1891, Bat married Emma. It was to be a lasting marriage, for Emma remained Bat's wife until the day he died, although she probably had some adjusting to do to put up with Bat's roving ways, and to be content to remain in the background while Bat garnered all the limelight. The marriage was without children.

Soon after their marriage, Bat and Emma went to Creede, Colorado, to try and cash in on the silver discovery there. Emma appeared content to give up her stage career while Bat continued to attend to business. He operated a gambling house and a restaurant in Creede until their return to Denver.

Back in Denver Bat tried his hand at handling prize-fighters. Boxing was new to him, but he was a fast learner acting at times as a second or as referee. Again he ran into political trouble. Otto Floto, prominent and wealthy publisher of the *Denver Post*, tried to use his influence to freeze out all competition when it came to promoting fights in Denver. This feud resulted in state legislation that brought to a halt both Bat's and Floto's activities in boxing.

Shortly thereafter President Theodore Roosevelt offered Bat the post of United States Marshal for the State of Oklahoma. Bat told him, "I am not the man for the job. Oklahoma is still woolly, and if I were marshal some youngster would want to try to put me out because of my reputation. I have taken my guns off, and I don't ever want to put them on again."

Bat still rankled at the way Floto had treated him, so one evening he trailed Floto from the restaurant. Near the *Denver Post* building Bat caught up with Floto, beating him severely about the head with his gold-headed cane . . . the cane the citizens of Dodge City had presented to Bat in 1885. This altercation worried the city officials, for they feared an all-out shooting match between Bat and Floto.

Chief of Police Hamilton Armstrong called Jim Marshall, an officer at Cripple Creek, Colorado, and asked for his help. It put Marshall on the spot, since he and Bat had been good friends through the years, and had stood shoulder to shoulder in a few shooting scrapes. However Marshall owed Armstrong, so he agreed to talk with Bat for his own good. Someone tipped off Bat about this arrangement. He wired Marshall that he would meet him behind Scholz Drugstore at ten o'clock the next morning.

Bat waited until eleven o'clock, but Marshall did not appear. Bat asked the storekeeper to inform anyone who asked for him that he had gone across the street to the bar in the Tabor Opera House.

Bat was just tipping his shot glass to his lips when he heard a voice say, 'Sorry I'm a little late, Bat?'

Masterson knew he was at a disadvantage. Marshall had slipped in through the side door and was at his side, pistol in hand, before he knew it.

Bat grinned. "Well, Jim, old friend, does this mean we have to fight?"

"Depends upon you, Bat."

"Meaning what?"

"Well, Bat, Denver is too big a town for you to hurrah. "Why don't you leave and let it go at that?"

"Leave? When?"

"Well, say late this afternoon, on the Burlington."

Humiliated as he was, Bat knew that wisdom was the better part of valor in a situation like this, so he agreed with the terms put forth by Marshall. Bat told Emma he was headed East and that he would send for her soon. Masterson left Denver that day, and no newspaper article ever appeared about it, the press apparently having been warned to 'lay off' the story.

Later Bat was appointed a federal marshal for the southern district of New York. This appointment Bat accepted, since it made Emma happy too. It was fair pay with security; they even got to visit with Roosevelt in the White House from time to time.

Bat remained in the marshal's office until offered a job by the Lewis brothers, newspapermen from New York. He became the sports editor for the *Morning Telegraph*. He also wrote a series of gunfighter stories for *Human Life* magazine. Although some believed they had been written to suit the reader rather than being the full truth, the stories were well received.

Masterson continued in the capacity of sports writer until October 25, 1921, the day he was found dead at his desk, still clutching his last bit of written material in his hand.

Hundreds of people attended Bat's funeral, among them William S. Hart, Damon Runyon, and Louella Parsons.

Emma Masterson lived another eleven years, ever faithful to her Bat, 'Knight of the Prairie'.

Frank Leslie,
Gunfighter

THE sound of an open-hand slap across the face echoed from the walls of the Oriental Saloon like a peal of thunder. A young man, his face redder from embarrassment than from the slap, crouched back against a chair, his hand to his cheek.

"Damn you, Leslie, you'll regret that! You'd best get your gun and come a-runnin', 'cause I aim to shoot you full o' holes for this insult, as well as for havin' a hand in the killin' o' my friend John Ringo."

"Go home and sleep it off, Billy. You're too drunk to think straight right now," said the mild-mannered man who had slapped the young man and who also was bartender at the Oriental.

The slap had resulted from a dispute about whether the young fellow should be served any more whiskey. The bartender did not believe he should be served, and his sentiments agreed with those of the lone customer who stood at the bar.

The young slappee was Billy Claiborne, once a good-natured cowboy who worked at the John Slaughter ranch in the San Pedro Valley, but who now thought he was a gunfighter because he had slain a man over a trivial matter during a card game. On paydays he would ride into Galeyville, Charleston, or Tombstone, the places frequented by Curly Bill, the Clantons, and the McLaury boys. In a spirit of drunken fun Billy's wild associates dubbed him 'Billy the Kid'. Of course, that sent Billy's ego hog-wild, and he boasted that he would make Billy the Kid Bonney look like a Sunday School teacher insofar as his lawless deeds were concerned.

Billy Claiborne quit his job at the Slaughter ranch and joined Curly Bill and his band of bandits. It was here that he also met that deadly gunfighter Johnny Ringo, whose background was as mysterious as that of any man who came west and wanted his past unknown. Billy and Ringo became as friendly as anyone could in such a group of robbers, and when Ringo's body was found under peculiar circumstances and a rumor circulated that Frank Leslie had killed him, it preyed upon Billy's mind. He felt it was his duty to avenge Johnny. However, it became a known fact that Leslie had nothing to do with the demise of Ringo. Many people believed that the famous gunman had committed suicide while on a drunken spree.

Recovering his composure, Billy strutted up to the bar and pounded his fist on the wood.

"I want whiskey, damn you, Leslie!"

Frank Leslie walked from behind the bar, caught Billy by the collar and walked him to the batwings.

"Get out, Billy. Come back when you're sober," said Leslie, as he turned away.

Billy left the saloon, his clouded mind still seething with rage over the insult. Suddenly he turned about-face and walked back into the building. Before he could even say a word, Leslie grabbed him by the collar again and pushed him into the street.

Claiborne glared and muttered, "I'll be back. Nobody shoves Billy the Kid around and gets away with it."

"Whenever you're ready," said the unarmed bartender.

At seven-thirty on the morning of November 14, 1882, a cowboy rushed into the Oriental, excitement beaming from his face.

"Frank, Claiborne's out in Allen Street. He's still all drunked up, but now he's carrying a rifle."

Leslie answered, "I'll see what I can do to appease him. We've always been good friends, and his attitude sure puzzles me."

With that Leslie removed his bar apron, took his .45 Colt Peacemaker from a drawer, and walked to a side door leading into Fifth Avenue.

He walked cautiously toward the young Claiborne, and when he was about thirty feet from him he called out, "Billy!"

The would-be gunslinger spun around, firing a shot from the hip. The bullet went wild. Then Billy threw the rifle to his shoulder to take more deliberate aim. At the same time the big .45

boomed, and the two shots sounded like one. Billy's second shot had also missed its mark, but Leslie's heavy slug tore through the young man's chest, and he collapsed in the dust and died.

Without a further look, Leslie spun on his heel, stepped back into the saloon, and continued dispensing whiskey as though nothing had happened.

Who was this small, wily man whose speed and accuracy with the six-gun could compete with any gunslinger of the day, and whose long, flowing moustache and wicked .45 Peacemaker caused comment wherever he went?

He was Frank Leslie, who, according to many reports, was born in Kentucky during the 1850s. Others have said that he was born in Galveston, Texas, in 1842, and that his real name was Kennedy. Leslie told friends that his mother's maiden name had been Leslie and that he had taken this name after he and his father had personal difficulties. His early training on the raw frontier had apparently included the art of handling firearms. He was so fast on the draw that many old-timers said he was as good as, or better than, most of the gunfighters who had roamed the West. Wyatt Earp, who claimed that Doc Holliday was the fastest gunman of the era, said many times that Leslie was the only man who was near Doc's equal on the fast draw.

During the 1870s Leslie was an army scout in the Dakotas and in Texas. He was stationed at the San Carlos Indian Reservation in Arizona in 1877, after having taken part in the campaign against Geronimo's renegades. He then decided to try his luck at prospecting. He had heard of Tombstone, that fabulous town on Goose Flats, where Scout Ed Schieffelin, unmindful of the warnings of Chief Army Scout Al Sieber, had gone into the mountains and discovered a lode of silver from which was spawned that wild and woolly town.

When Leslie rode into Tombstone in 1880 he was still wearing his fringed buckskin scout's jacket. His brown hair was shoulder length, and he wore two six-guns draped from his lean hips. Many of the men of the town called him a ham and also dubbed him Buckskin Frank. However, those who questioned his skill soon learned their mistake. Beneath that fetching smile and gaudy dress lay a vicious and passionate man who could back up his hand with one of the fastest draws of any man in Tombstone.

He staked his mine carefully and probably could have become a rich man had he paid more attention to it. However, the large mining interests in Tombstone found a loophole concerning Leslie's mine and had annexed it to their own. Legal action proved fruitless, and Frank lost his holdings to the powerful Tombstone combines. It did not seem to affect him greatly, for he soon opened the Cosmopolitan Hotel on Allen Street, in direct competition with the Commercial Hotel, whose bartender was one Mike Killeen.

May Killeen, the raven-haired, blue-eyed estranged wife of Mike, was a maid at the Cosmopolitan Hotel, where Leslie struck up a close friendship with her. Mike Killeen had threatened to kill any man who dared show his wife attention. It was soon apparent that Mrs. Killeen and Frank Leslie had fallen in love.

On the night of June 22, 1880, the

trouble happened, and George Perine, a close friend of Frank's, became involved in the romantic triangle. Perine and Leslie had gone to the dance at the Cook-Vizina building, and May Killeen joined them when the dance was over. The trio then walked to the Cosmopolitan Hotel, where Leslie and May sat down on the front porch while Perine went into the bar for a drink. Perine saw Mike Killeen approaching and yelled a warning to Leslie.

"Take that, you son-of-a-bitch!" yelled Killeen as he fired at Leslie.

His first shot grazed Leslie's head. The second also grazed the top of his head. Leslie was not carrying his gun at the time, but he did have a small revolver. Before he could draw this, Killeen was upon him, beating him over the head with his heavy revolver. Leslie grabbed his weapon from his pocket and shot his assailant twice. Killeen fell away, running into the hotel and down a hallway.

Frank Leslie was arrested by Officer Bennett, and Perine was taken by City Marshal Fred White. Killeen died five days later after having given a statement to a male nurse named E.T. Packwood, who reported that Killeen swore that it had been Perine who fired the fatal shot.

On August 6 Buckskin Frank Leslie and May Killeen were married by Judge Reilly at the Cosmopolitan Hotel. It was also about this time that one W.T Lowry swore out a warrant for the arrest of George Perine, charging him with the murder of Mike Killeen.

After hearing all the testimony, Judge Reilly decided to hold Perine over for the grand jury. Unable to raise the bail, Perine was taken to Tucson by Deputy Sheriff Wyatt Earp for safekeeping. However he was released when the October grand jury failed to return an indictment against him.

In 1881 Leslie became head bartender at the Oriental Saloon, the property of Billy Harris. There he met the Earps, Bat Masterson, and Luke Short, but he never became a member of the Earp gang. It was about this time that the feud between the Earps and Johnny Behan, sheriff of Cochise County, began to warm up. It was difficult to remain neutral, yet Frank Leslie, with an artful tact, managed to do so in a pro-Earp saloon and though drinking with Earp's enemies.

Things changed in Tombstone after 1881. Leslie changed his wearing attire from his famous buckskins to a Prince Albert coat. He no longer wore his famous Peacemaker in a hip holster; this revolver was now on the side of his hip, held in a fancy, silver-engraved clip on the side of his belt. The slaughter at the O.K. Corral on October 26, 1881, had touched off the spark that brought the Behan-Earp feud to its peak. Wyatt Earp and his gang left Tombstone on March 21, 1882; later Sheriff Behan was removed from office.

The middle 1880s saw the silver mines flooded and an exodus of citizens, until only a few hundred remained. Among those who left Tombstone was Frank Leslie, for in June 1883 he again joined the Apache scouts. But later he linked up with Milt Joyce in operating his Magnolia Ranch twenty miles from Tombstone. They built up a large herd in the two years before Joyce sold his interest in the ranch to Leslie and moved to San Francisco.

In May 1885, when Geronimo led his braves off the reservation for the last time, Leslie again acted as a scout until the end of June. He returned to the Magnolia Ranch in the Swisshelms Mountains after that and undertook to build up his herd.

After seven years of married life with Frank Leslie, May started divorce proceedings against him. She alleged that he was unfaithful, that he had beaten her that he had failed to provide for her and that she was fearful of her life when he would place her against a wall and shoot her profile in bullets. Judge William H. Barnes granted the divorce on September 3, 1887. Two years later May married a man named Alex Durward, and they moved to California, where she died on March 27, 1947.

It was not long after their divorce that Frank Leslie took up with Mollie Williams, also called Diamond Annie, a former Red Light District siren and entertainer at the Bird Cage Theatre. Mollie and Frank lived at the Magnolia

Ranch for two years. Then one night — the date was July 10, 1889 — he killed her.

They had arrived home from Tombstone and had spent the day fighting. Both had been drinking heavily. In the evening there was another fight. Leslie knocked Mollie down several times. After that he left on his horse saying he was going to William Reynolds's ranch to kill him. Reynolds was not at home.

When Leslie returned to his ranch, he found Mollie sitting on the porch with Jim Neal, a seventeen-year-old youth who had drifted into town and whom Leslie had hired as a ranch hand. (In some reports the boy's name is listed as Jimmy Hibbs or Jim Hughes.) Insanely jealous at the sight of his ranch hand and Mollie engaged in pleasant conversation, Leslie raced into the house, grabbed a revolver, and fired at Mollie. She staggered to her feet, tottered to the side of the house, and fell at the back door dead.

Young Neal was petrified. Leslie jammed the pistol into his ribs and fired again. The boy thought first it was a make-believe incident. When he felt the blood trickling down his side, he bolted and ran. He managed to escape in the darkness, making his way to the Reynolds's ranch. The rancher summoned Dr. Goodfellow from Tombstone to treat the wounded lad and two days later took him in a spring wagon to Tombstone. He informed the sheriff's office that he had seen Leslie at the Abbott ranch on the way in.

Four deputies found Leslie near the Four Bar Ranch. He was riding toward Tombstone with two other men, telling them that Neal had slain his wife and that he had to kill the boy. When he walked into the sheriff's office and saw the boy resting on a cot, he recognized he had walked into a trap.

Frank Leslie was found guilty of his crime and was sentenced to serve a term of twenty-five years in the state prison at Yuma. He was received at the prison on December 10, 1889, and booked as convict #632. He was five feet seven and a quarter inches tall, and weighed 135 pounds. He was permitted to retain his #5 boots, for the prison could not find shoes small enough to fit him. He was also given the privilege of retaining his luxuriant moustache instead of being clean-shaven as required of other prisoners.

Frank Leslie proved to be a model prisoner. About four years after the start of his term he was instrumental in preventing a prison break. His action incidentally saved the lives of several prison guards. At one time a reporter from the *San Francisco Chronicle* visited Leslie and asked for his story of the killing of his wife. Leslie gave him an entirely original version, which appeared in the *Chronicle*.

Mrs. Belle Stowell, after reading Leslie's account, started to write him and continued to do so until his release. In 1896 Leslie's case was brought up before the territorial governor accompanied by a fat portfolio of letters of recommendation and petitions for his release. On November 17, 1896, Governor Franklin granted Leslie a full pardon.

On December 1, 1896, Leslie married his benefactor, Mrs. Stowell. He took a job as a bodyguard for Professor Dumble, a geologist who was going to Mexico to check the coal mines of the Southern Pacific Railroad. Several years later he headed for the Klondike gold fields, and it was reported that he made a small fortune there. Nothing more is heard of his wife, so apparently he deserted her somewhere along the way.

In 1911 Leslie was working in a saloon in Oakland, California, borrowing on occasion from some of his old friends. Intensive research into the legend of Frank Leslie reveals, indeed, that he was working in a saloon in California as late as 1924. Curiously, it seems that the bartender there at the time was Jim Neal, the young man Leslie had almost killed the night he shot his wife Molly.

Before long, however he stole the owner's revolver and left. This gun was subsequently identified as the one alongside the skeleton of a man found in the desert, readily accepted as the bones of Frank Leslie. Some said he committed suicide where the pistol and bones were discovered.

In 1948 a man known as Barney McCoy died in a hospital in San Diego — having claimed toward the end he was really Frank Leslie. No one will ever know for sure.

Half-Million-Dollar Robbery

My thanks to Pat Wagner, editor of Western Publications, for permission to rewrite the story of the Half-Million-Dollar Robbery. It was told me by Leona Montgomery Roberts, daughter of Jack Montgomery (no relation to the John Montgomery of this book). She died a few years ago, last of the pioneer women of Oregon. At her passing I wrote a short article for a national magazine to honor her as 'one of the finest ladies that I ever had the good fortune to be associated with'.— W.M.

THERE was only one way to stop Jack Montgomery, a driver who couldn't be robbed. He simply blew up the road as he went along. Without question he was the boldest stage driver on the Wild Frontier. Yet even he was robbed of half-a-million dollars in gold dust in the worst stage robbery in history.

Jack was about six feet tall, weighed two hundred pounds, was blond, a jovial person, well liked by young and old. During his waking hours he was never seen without a big black cigar poked in his mouth, puffing smoke like an engine. This habit saved his life during the great robbery.

His stage had never been robbed, although attempts had frequently been made. Once a troop of Indians spread out across the road in front of him. When he saw what they were up to, he whipped up his eight-horse team into a full gallop and crashed through them, then outran those who survived his onslaught. With his two guards blasting away, the Indians who followed soon gave up.

Jack's wild abandon saved the day many times. He would gallop an eight- or a ten-horse team through high narrow mountain roads where most drivers feared to walk a team.

In May 1867 another man and Jack sat in front of a freight office enjoying the spring weather discussing what they would like to do on a fine day like this. Fishing was out, as freight had piled up during the past winter and had to be moved at once. There would be no time off and a lot of extra driving.

At this time Jack had a regular stage run between Eugene and Striped Horse, Oregon. As the two men sat talking, a boy walked up and told Jack that M.J.J. Comstock, superintendent of the Oregon and California Stage Company, wanted to see him.

"Now," said Jack, "I wonder what the hell he wants. If he wants me to drive back to Striped Horse today, I have something to tell him."

When he reached the office, he was asked to sit down.

"Mr. Montgomery," began Mr. Howard, "I'll make this brief, and to the point. I am informed that you are the only man who can accomplish this task. This last winter there has been a great gold strike, and we have managed thus far to keep it quiet, especially to the outside world. We have even kept it away from most people hereabouts. It has to be kept quiet until

232

we get out this shipment of gold. Then we'll have fifty thousand men in here in no time."

"There is a half million in gold dust, and you'll have the largest stage available. Instead of taking it to San Francisco as usual, we are going to take it from Jacksonville to Portland and ship it from there to Frisco by boat. This should throw off any would-be robbers. They'll be watching the road and not the boat. You will have a full complement of passengers and a ten-horse team. The passengers will tend to allay suspicion. If you accept this assignment, you will be paid $150 for the trip plus a $100 bonus.

This amount was no less than a small fortune to a stage driver.

Jack said to Mr. Howard, "I'll drive that stage to the moon for $250. Just give me fifteen minutes and I'll be ready."

A day or two later when Jack returned from Striped Horse, he was notified to be ready to take off the following day at daybreak.

When you mention gold, most people think of California. Yet some of the greatest strikes were made in Oregon. In those days there was very little law and order. A town usually hired a marshal who policed the small-town streets and did nothing more. Stage companies hired the best marksmen to ride the stages, also the best drivers, dedicated to delivering the cargo properly.

The half-million in gold was fetched in at night to the stage storage shed. It was sewn into small leather bags stored inside iron-bound wooden boxes. These were placed at various places underneath the stage.

(Many have doubted the ability of one stage to carry this much weight [about 10,000 pounds], but the largest Concord stages could carry all that could be placed on them, along with several passengers, provided they could be pulled, and this stage had a ten-horse team.) When the stage was pulled from the shed, the team was hitched and the passengers on board. Two shotgun guards mounted their stations, one up front with Jack and one on the boot. Later they were to pick up several horse guards.

Jack came out as usual — a bottle of

whiskey in one hand and a box of cigars in the other. He wore two pistols and a large knife in his belt. He mounted to his place while stage hands held the horses. He adjusted himself to the seat and fastened his safety belt — without these safety belts a driver or guard could be thrown from the stage. As the stage pulled out, Howard and Comstock were on hand to wish Jack luck, along with the usual flock of Jacksonville residents.

Howard remarked to Comstock, "Do you allow your drivers to drink on the job?"

Comstock replied, with a wide smile on his face, "In Jack's case, yes. All we have to worry about is that the outlaws don't find out what he drinks."

Jack looked things over, gathered the lines, kicked off the foot brake. He then uncoiled his twenty-foot bullwhip, threw it back and forward, made it crack like a .45 – .70 rifle. The horses hit their collars as one and were soon in a full gallop.

Once they had pulled out, Jack's shotgun rider, Sam, could contain himself no longer.

"Jack," he asked, "I'd sure as hell like

to know what this stage is carrying to attract so much attention."

Jack pulled on his cigar a few times before answering, "Sam, I have known you for a long time, and I believe you can be trusted as far as any man can be where half a million in gold is concerned."

Sam became so excited that he would have fallen from the stage had it not been for his belt.

"Gold! I knowed damn well we had gold, but half a million — good God! I didn't know there was that much in the whole world."

Jack was reassuring. "We are pretty safe from thieves," he said, "because the officials have been real secretive about this shipment. So don't worry. Just keep that gun handy."

Sam surveyed the area thoughtfully. "I know you are just talking to make conversation, Jack. You know good and well, official or otherwise, that where that much gold is concerned no man can be trusted entirely."

Both knew the shipment could not have been kept completely secret.

The first stage stop was Jump-Off Joe's

Place, and Jack told the passengers to remain inside, for they were stopping only long enough to change teams. From here they roared through Rogue River country, as wild and as rough as the road. Jack didn't slow down. He kept the team at a full gallop. Now and then he would crack that long whip to let the horses know he wanted all they could give.

When they reached Grace Creek Station, he told the passengers they had twenty minutes to eat and take care of other needs. The stage men remained with the coach and ate outside while the team was being changed. This was wild country, and they could not take a chance of being away a single minute.

When all was ready, with the passengers once more aboard, Jack cracked his long whip, and they were off again. One passenger remarked, "If that man don't slow down, we'll all be killed. I wish he'd quit cracking that whip. Sounds like we were being fired at."

After some time Sam looked ahead and yelled to Jack, "Look ahead! Robbers, sure as hell!"

He saw four mounted men waiting for the stage and brought up his rifle, ready to fight.

Jack told him, "Put down your gun. Those are guards to see us through the roughest part of the trip."

Sam was relieved. As the stage roared past, the four riders fell in behind.

It required good riding to keep up with a stage driven by Jack, more especially, this stage. Many a band of Indians had been outrun by good stage horses and a good driver. The next stop would be at Canyon Creek. The road here was barely wide enough to slow down. Jack went through it like a bat out of hell.

Now and then Sam would shout, "For God's sake, watch those rocks!"

Sam had traveled this road many times and knew of several stages that had gone over the side. It was dangerous, and he knew it. But he didn't slow down. Now and then, when he hit a level spot, he would take a swig from his bottle.

They stopped at Canyon Creek Station long enough only to change horses. Then they were off again, down through the Missouri bottoms, where the going was

238

smooth, then back into the mountains, where the road was worse than at any other time. Several times they had to stop and remove large rocks from the road. When they reached Big Rock Station, the passengers were again allowed twenty minutes to eat and stretch their legs.

Jack and the guards ate stew on the porch while the others ate inside the building. Here Jack told the guards that they would travel all night; he wanted to get rid of his freight as quickly as possible. Sam begged him to slow down. "You can't make it over that road at night," he warned. To no avail. They left on time.

Jack had informed the mounted guards that he would give them a signal about five miles out, meaning they could return. By that time, he was sure, the danger would be over. He said, "Had outlaws been going to strike, they'd have done so by now, where the timber was heavy and the going really rough.

He could not have been more wrong.

The guards, as instructed, left the coach about five miles from the last station. Jack had lit the lamps on the outside of the coach. He didn't want to stop unless absolutely necessary. The stage was compelled to slow down considerably as it climbed Roberts Hill. The road was being worked on and was in bad condition. When the stage crossed Wild Cat Bridge, the noise from the loose boards could be heard five miles away. And when it passed Umpqua Falls the passengers thought they were running into a thunderstorm.

"It won't be long now," Jack promised. "In about fifteen minutes we'll be in Mountain Home Station, and we'll stop and rest for a while."

He did not suspect that on a hillside half a mile away sat three hard-looking men. One had a fuse in his hand, another a lighted torch. At that point, the road ran between two high, steep hills — a deep cut in the mountain made to improve the road.

Jack and Sam were looking ahead into the darkness just before reaching the cut when they heard a boom, then a blasting flash. Jack tried in vain to check the team. When he saw that the horses had panicked, he jerked out his knife, cut his safety belt, and jumped. He had no choice. It was jump or die with the coach. Sam failed to cut his belt and was crushed to death. He had dropped his knife. It was found later some distance from his body.

George Kelley, the guard on the hind boot, had already unfastened his belt, ready to jump if Jack put the stage over the brink, which was about a thousand feet to the bottom. He jumped at the flash, hit the road hard, and rolled in the dust unhurt. He said afterward that he got to his feet and ran as fast as he could in the opposite direction, then off the side of the road until he fell exhausted in the brush.

As he lay there he counted twenty-one mules pass by, with a mounted man in front and one in back. Each mule was tied to the tail of the one behind it. George stayed hidden until the mule train returned, accompanied now by six riders. He knew they were carrying off the gold. After they were out of sight, he returned to the stage and found it almost covered from the rockslide and passengers inside yelling. When his efforts to free them failed, he told them he would go to the station for help — it was only a short distance away.

The dynamite bomb had been set off a little too soon, but the plan had worked. Had the stage gone a little farther, it would have been completely smashed by the rock-slide. Luckily, the horses did not quite make it to the cut. The stage, on its side on the brink of a steep drop, was only partly covered with rocks.

At the station George found Jack Montgomery on a cot with the stage manager's wife, Alma Redding, sewing up a long gash in his belly.

She said, "Jack came in holding his insides in his two hands. He told me about the avalanche that crushed the stage, and then he fell to the floor."

He had lost much blood and was badly wounded. She had doctored many a wounded man and was doing the best she could for Jack.

George seated himself at a table, poured himself a stiff drink, and tried to visualize what had occurred. When Jack regained consciousness, they talked for a short time. Then Jack fell asleep.

Alma Redding told George that when she heard the explosion, she ordered two stage hands to investigate. They refused to go until two more men arrived. When the four reached the stage, they found three passengers and eight horses dead. They cut loose the two live horses and rescued five passengers. One rider returned and told Alma to make a place for them to lie down, for they were all in bad shape.

Every ounce of gold was missing. The robbery had been a success.

Once Jack had recovered sufficiently to make a statement, he said: "When I saw the light from the blast, I tried to check the horses, but they went crazy and ran straight into the sliding rock. I jerked my knife and cut my belt and jumped, but first I called for Sam to jump. I went down that steep incline about a hundred feet and hung on a scrub pine. Rock was sliding down all around me, and I hung onto the pine. Fortunately none of the rocks struck me. I was on a solid rock a few feet above the slide."

He had looked up the slope and seen several figures around the stage. From their talk he knew they were outlaws. He pulled out his pistol and fired at them. He apparently hit one, for he heard him scream.

One of them said, "There's one that ain't dead, sure as hell."

They fired several shots in Jack's direction, which missed him. Then he felt someone in back of him. He turned and tried to fire, but his gun snapped — it was empty. The man behind him struck at him with a razor-sharp hatchet taken from the stage. Jack took the blow across his midsection. When he felt the blood gush, he knew he had been hit. He grabbed at the man, but he was no match for him, he was too weak. He realized he still had his cigar in his mouth. He took the cigar in his free hand and jammed it into the man's eye. The man yelled and dropped his hatchet. Jack picked up the hatchet and struck the man over the head. The body slid down the bank a short distance and didn't move again, so Jack figured he had killed him.

It was a bright moonlit night, and Jack could see for some distance. He pulled off his shirt and saw that his intestines were protruding from the wound in his belly. He placed both hands over the cut and slowly made his way to the stage station. Once there, he collapsed on the floor. Alma Redding began to work on his wound.

Jack eventually recovered and returned to his job of driving a stage, but he never fully got over the loss of the half-million in gold. The man 'who couldn't be stopped' had failed. He talked to the vigilantes several times, trying to come up with something that would lead them to the robbers. A posse from Roseburg, investigating the robbery, followed the mule tracks to the Umpqua River. There they gave up. The mules had followed the stream. The posse could not find out where they had left the river.

Some time after the vigilante committee was notified of four men in a cave near the scene of the stage robbery in the Siskiyou Mountains. They swooped down on the cave, captured the four men, and found four sacks of gold dust. The captives denied any knowledge of the crime. They said they had entered the cave to get out of the bad weather and, to their surprise, had found the gold there.

The vigilantes were not satisfied with their story, and the four men were hanged.

Today this kind of justice may seem cruel and inhuman, but in those wild days it worked. The Oregon vigilantes were the most effective in the West. They rid the state of many hardened criminals.

Jack Montgomery continued to drive the stagecoach until the railroad took over his run. Turning then to quieter pursuits, he homesteaded 160 acres in the agate district of Jackson County and ran a general store. In October 1878 he married the daughter of a southern Oregon pioneer, Burril B. Griffin.

In 1910 Jack died at Eagle Point, Oregon, at the age of seventy-nine. One of the last, and probably best, stage drivers of the Old West had gone to his reward.

The Ludlow Massacre

WALTER MONTGOMERY (father of Wayne) was born in Santa Fe, New Mexico, in 1874. He moved to Tombstone with his father and the rest of the family in 1879, and lived there until he was sixteen years old. He left home then to become a professional prizefighter. He had gotten plenty of practice by that time from fighting town toughs in the streets of Tombstone.

He was bumming his way on the railroad in Kansas when he stopped in a small town and went into a saloon to get a little free lunch. In the saloon he saw a Negro giant training for a fight. The promoters offered a hundred dollars to any man who could beat him.

Walter had never seen a boxing glove. But, he had beaten men he figured as good as this one. So he challenged this fighter. The man's handler said Walter was too small, so Walter agreed to fight him winner-take-all. Usually the loser got a small purse.

The stage was set. They roped off some trees because they had no ring. They gave out instructions and rang the bell. The fighters blasted each other for ten rounds. When the bell for the eleventh round rang, the Negro refused to come out. He had had enough of this wild man half his size. So Walter got the hundred dollars. To him this was a streak of fortune; in fact, it was to everybody. He never weighed over a hundred and fifty pounds, was short and heavy set, but he had the punch of a heavyweight. He flattened many men in the first round.

He went to live in Joplin, Missouri, and there he met an aspiring young boxer named Jim Ferns. Jim was born on January 20,1874, in Wier City, Kansas, a wide place in the road. They worked together in the mines and fought in the ring whenever the chance came.

Ferns wanted Walter to go to Chicago with him and try for the big time, but Walter thought he could do better in the mines. Ferns made it to Chicago, sought out the promoters of major boxing matches, and asked for a chance. He explained how many men he had whipped. They had never heard of him, nor of the men he had whipped. He kept after them. Finally they said they would put him in a four-round prelim. He wanted no prelim — he wanted to fight. He continued pestering them until one day they gave in. There was a fine middleweight named Billy Edwards working out in the club. He was on his way to a fight with the middleweight champ.

They told Ferns they wanted to see him in action, which pleased him beyond words. They told Edwards privately to work him over good, for he was a bother and they wanted to get rid of him, to send him back to the Kansas mines.

The fight started, and Edwards found his opponent was no setup. In the second round Ferns knocked him colder than a wedge. The audience went wild. Some newsmen were present and saw Ferns blast this man cold. The promoters assured them that this was a fluke punch, that it couldn't happen again in a hundred years.

Pressure was brought to bear and Ferns was matched with Edwards in a real fight in 1896. As before, Ferns knocked him out cold. He was written up big as the rube from Kansas who had beaten the great Billy Edwards with ease. After that he was known as 'Rube Ferns'.

From then on he fought them all, and in 1898 won the welterweight championship of the world. He beat one of he greatest fighters of all time, Mysterious Billy Smith. Rube Ferns had Smith cut so badly that in the twenty-first round Smith quit. Some time later Ferns lost the title to Matty Matthews, won it back, then lost it to the great welter, the original Joe Wolcott, a Negro and an outstanding one. Wolcott was born in the West Indies in 1873 and fought his first fight in 1890. He was killed in an auto accident in Ohio in October 1935.

Walter Montgomery fought Ferns twice, the first fight on December 11,1898, in Chicago. Both were ten rounders for the title and Walter lost both times. The record reads one draw and one knockout. This is inaccurate, for Ferns was awarded the second fight by a decision.

Walter's greatest achievement was his knockout of Hugo Kelley in two rounds at Chicago. He fought under several names — Buck Montgomery, Bob Montgomery, and his own name, Walter. When he grew too old for the fight business, he returned to the mines, a sorry way to make a living. He had a son named Walter and one named Wayne and two other sons and two daughters. His son named Wayne was born in Petersburg, Illinois. The older brother was Walter the younger one John, and afterward the two sisters, Vera and Mable, who are still living.

Walter Montgomery knew he would never earn a decent living working in a coal mine, and undertook a means to better his situation. With the aid of a teacher he studied day and night. It paid off. He was offered a white-collar job as an organizer for the United Mine Workers and was ordered to Pittsburg, Pennsylvania. He was given this job because he could talk intelligently and also because he could flatten a man with one punch. He left his family at a wide place in the road called Tice, now extinct, and after a few months he sent his wife money to outfit the children and for train fare.

Heretofore his wife had made all the family clothing, but she no longer had time. With the money he sent she marched the six children to the company store and bought them suits left over from the Civil War. Those children were a rare sight to the upper class on that train. They had, almost literally, to lead the oldest son onto the train with a pair of plow handles.

At long last the family boarded the midnight special for Springfield, where they had to take the through train for Pittsburg. Only their mother had ever ridden on a train before. For the kids this was a great experience — four ornery boys, who, before they reached their destination, nearly drove several trainmen to an early grave.

After boarding the last train and getting settled, they noticed that their young preacher was on the same train and in the same car. Wayne hated him with a childish passion because he had ratted on him for putting only one cent in the collection plate when he had been given

252

five cents — young Wayne was saving four cents for chewing gum. Besides, the preacher had been seen making calf eyes at a young girl in the congregation, and he was not overly fond of a boy with suspicions about him.

The preacher, weary from overwork, reared back in his seat and fell asleep. Young Wayne got hold of one of his mother's hatpins and stealthily slithered beneath the seats until he come to the preacher's seat. There was a wide crack in that seat, ideal for his intention. He took dead aim and with all his strength speared the preacher in the back side with that hatpin. The poor man jumped ten feet into the air and screamed like a wounded Apache. All the other passengers looked at him as though he had gone daft. Although Wayne was suspected, the old conductor swore that the boy was asleep at the time. The preacher remained standing the remainder of the trip. When he disembarked at Springfield he favored one hip, and young Wayne felt he had evened the score.

In the course of the trip one day the conductor came through and saw the porter Sam on his knees going through the coach. He asked, "Sam, what in tarnation are you doing on the floor? You'll get your white suit dirty."

Sam replied, "Boss, they's a air leak sommers, I c'n hear it now and again."

The conductor told Sam to keep up the good work. What had transpired was that Wayne's young brother John was on his knees near a window, pretending to drive the train and making a hissing sound through his teeth. It drove Sam to distraction. When Sam was at the other end of the coach John would make that sound, and that set Sam searching again. It was several hours before Sam discovered what was happening. From then on every time he passed one of us he said, "Po' white trash."

Mother told us, "Pay him no mind. We can't he'p 'cause we're white."

At last the family reached their destination, to the great pleasure of all the trainmen, especially Sam. As they walked down the steps leaving the train, there stood Sam, hat in hand, waiting to be rewarded for his honest and faithful service to the passengers. He stooped to retrieve a nickel tip he'd just been given and dropped. As he exposed his backside young Wayne came along, still holding his mother's hatpin, and he speared Sam. Sam jumped onto two old men, knocking them to the platform, and he yelled like a wild Indian, and ran around holding his backside with both hands. When his mother saw what her son had done, she grabbed a slab from a crate and saw to it that he would take his meals standing for a week.

Walter met his family, dressed like a lawyer, and led them to an auto, a National touring car. The children felt great blasting through town at the high rate of about fifteen miles per hour. They had a driver and were taken to a flat, as it was called then. It had hot and cold water and an inside privy. Their mother had never dreamed of such things.

The family lived there for two years, the greatest time of their life. The mother had a car at her disposal any time she wanted to go anywhere. She had a credit account at a department store and, by her standards, lived like a queen. Then came the blast. Walter was ordered to

Walsenburg, Colorado, where a civil war had been in progress for many years, a war between the miners and the coal operators.

In Walsenburg they found a house near the center of town. The situation there was grim; murder was as common as snow on the nearby mountains. The sheriff of Huerfano County had ruled this county with an iron hand under the direction of the coal operators for twenty years without a proper election. He had under him about three hundred deputies, as they were referred to; actually they were mine guards paid by the operators. When a man got out of line he was driven out of town or killed.

Shortly after Walter's family arrived a newsman from Denver moved in to collect material about conditions there. One night he answered a knock on his door and was killed by a shotgun blast. No arrests were made, for Jeff Farr the sheriff, did not want any publicity.

The situation existing at that time and place defies comprehension. John D. Rockefeller owned this vast empire. He had every lawman, the National

Guard, judges, lawyers, everybody of any importance all on his payroll — the richest man on earth, who ruled his realm so that the miners lived like slaves. The miners had for twenty years tried to break this yoke of bondage that enslaved them and their families.

Rockefeller made his own laws. He defied state and federal laws. Miners were paid in scrip, a violation of federal law. This scrip could be spent only in a company-owned establishment. The saloons, general stores, all the houses were company property. The mines had no safety devices. The National Guard, so called, was made up of imported thugs and attired in the uniform of the army to do the bidding of John D.

Walter Montgomery moved into an office in Walsenburg surrounded by guards of the union. What follows is the personal recollection of Wayne Montgomery, Walter's second son.

★ ★ ★

Soon after our arrival father homesteaded 320 acres of land sixteen miles west of

Walsenburg and six miles north of La Veta, and he moved the family there for safety's sake. He had a log house built for us to live in.

One day a lieutenant of the National Guard stopped father on the street and began giving him orders. He could either comply or get out of town. Father blasted him with a punch that put him out cold. This lieutenant was named Linderfelt, a beast of the lowest order.

While riding with father once in the car furnished him by the union, we saw three dead miners along the road west of Walsenburg. They had foolishly announced that they were leaving. Another was killed at La Veta for the same reason. Between 1900 and 1914 about a hundred miners had been killed, with no arrests made.

My father spent much time at Ludlow. He worked with Louis Tikas, the little Greek, who had as much guts as my father. There was only a handful of union men present, against about 200 armed guards, but father and Tikas gave them as much trouble as possible.

Father had one terrible fight at Ludlow.

258

Linderfelt had ordered one of his thugs to pick a fight with father and figured he would have his other boys to aid in this affair. But he was wrong. About fifty miners showed up, and the lieutenant wasn't ready to kill them yet. He lacked orders. A giant of a man jumped father on one of the streets, and they went at it. He was big and tough as nails, but father blasted him from all directions. Finally, after some time, he was knocked out with a shot to his belly. This only caused a much worse feeling by the guards towards the miners and their families.

In this vast area there were about fifty coal mines, surrounded by barbed wire and guarded by thugs in uniform. Towers were built on hills and used to survey the roads for strangers. Many of these towers remain to this day. Every mine worked 800 miners.

The first winter father decided to move us into a small village because life on the ranch was too rough in winter and there were no schools in our area. We moved into Ojo, now extinct, about five miles west of La Veta.

One morning father was called to settle

a dispute at the mine. When he arrived there he found several hundred miners in an argument with guards. A man named Bill Donnelly was accompanying father. A big two-hundred-pound guard walked up to father and ordered him to get the hell out of the mine area. Father knocked him down. He got up and was knocked down again, four times in all. Whereupon the guard tried to pull a club out of the frozen ground. Father hit him on the back of his head, and the big man was out. That stopped the trouble for the time being.

When Jeff Farr, the sheriff, was told about the beating of this guard, he ordered father and Donnelly arrested. The plan was to get them out of Ojo and kill them. The plan failed.

That night after dark a deputy knocked on our door and informed father that he and Donnelly were under arrest. Father shoved him out and closed the door. I recall this incident very distinctly, for I was thirteen years old. Guards surrounded our house and called for father and Donnelly to come out or they would shoot up the house. Father had more guts than a mine mule. He called a truce with the guards.

John McDowell lived across the street from us, and father escorted mother my oldest brother and me to his house, then returned and waited for the results.

There were four men in our house at that time, including Donnelly. Donnelly had his right hand in a sling. He had broken a bone in his hand on the head of a guard. He took down his single-action .45 and accidently fired it through the floor. The guards thought war had been declared and shot into the house several times. Donnelly told father he was going to slip out the back way where he could see those bastards. He put on father's coat and hat, stepped out onto the back porch, and looked into a cocked revolver held by a guard.

The guard fired, and the bullet struck Donnelly in the neck, going completely through and out the back. The guard backed off, and Donnelly, using his left hand, shot and killed this guard. The other guards scattered like chickens.

After the guards left, we came back home. There was no doctor in Ojo, so mother doctored Donnelly as best she could. I recall her poking a piece of white cloth into Donnelly's wound from the front and the back. He sat in a chair and had my oldest brother roll cigarettes for him. Jeff Farr and a doctor came the next day about 10:00 A.M. Donnelly was removed to a hospital in Walsenburg, and father was taken to jail. He was out in a short time, for Farr had to be careful. Donnelly's killing of the guard made the outside papers.

When Donnelly was released from the hospital, he served fourteen months in jail, awaiting trial. He was acquitted. A few days later he was killed from ambush near Big Four, Colorado.

Two mornings after Donnelly had killed the guard, father returned to the same pit head. The big man he had fought with sneaked up behind him and struck him with a blackjack several times, but failed to knock him down. Father managed to get the man's thumb in his mouth and almost chewed it off, causing the man to drop the blackjack. Then father managed to get his hands in the man's hair shoved his head back over a prop pile, and for several minutes fired punch after punch into the man's belly. When he released him, the man almost dead fell unconscious to the ground. This occurred in the presence of 300 miners, afraid to raise their hands out of fear instilled in them by Jeff Farr.

In what you are about to read so many are killed and wounded that to some this story may seem unbelievable and incomprehensible, an exaggeration or even a fabrication. Alas, it is the bare truth. Colorado history will bear me out.

For a time killings began to slow down. Instead, men were sentenced to life imprisonment by the same judge and the same jury. A good friend of my family, Charley Haines (his son still lives in Walsenburg), was arrested for murder a man who never carried a gun in his life. John Lawson, the man in charge of this field of the United Mine Workers, was sentenced to life in prison. He also had never carried a gun. These were frame-ups, as were numerous others. Murder was not out yet by far. The worst was yet to come.

After every means were exhausted to get some sort of settlement with John D., one of peace, the miners were called out on strike. Hitherto, when they attempted to strike, they were driven back to work by the elements — terribly cold winters, with no place to live and no food.

This was in the fall of 1913. The union set up tents, sent to them from all over the United States, to house these unfortunate victims of circumstances. At Ludlow the tent colony resembled a vast city, which it actually was. Hundreds of tents could be seen everywhere. They were laid out in the form of streets. On either side a deep ditch was dug to carry off water during flash floods, which were quite common in this area. These ditches proved a godsend later on and saved hundreds of lives.

The people in these camps were given food, shelter, medical attention, and clothing by the union. As soon as the strike was called, the operators evicted every miner from his company-owned house into a cold winter. Had it not been for the tent colonies the miners and their families would have perished.

A National Guard company was sent in and camped on a hill west of the Ludlow camp under the command of Lieutenant Linderfelt, the worst bunch of scum ever gathered in one spot. (The National Guard of that day is not to be confused with the National Guard of today. Today's Guard is a fine, outstanding organization.)

The Guard was supposedly sent in to protect the miners and their families. They were actually sent there to browbeat the miners into returning to work. [They rode up and down the tent colony streets on horseback, ran children off the streets, ordered people to remain inside their tents. The only place people were permitted to go was to the railroad pumphouse for water. This great well was drilled there to supply trains with water and it was housed in a building called the pumphouse. The guards turned this colony into a prison camp. The union had no way to keep them out, for its members were outnumbered fifty to one. The guards allowed no one to leave without express permission from Lieutenant Linderfelt.

The miners had a leader named Louis Tikas, a Greek who weighed about a hundred and twenty-five pounds. He was pure hell. He defied the guards at every turn and cursed them to their faces. They hated him and wanted to get him out of the way.

One day General Chase, the commanding officer of the Colorado National Guard, paid the camp a visit. He spoke to a sixteen-year-old girl, and she called him an S.O.B. He kicked her in the breast as he sat in the saddle. The horse reared and dumped him into the street in the sight of many women and children. He ordered, "Ride them down!" Four women were slashed with sabers.

History records no darker chapter than the infamous Ludlow Massacre that culminated on April 20, 1914.

There are a few left who survived that massacre, but it is difficult to get a clear picture of what occurred that day. It was so horrible that most of its remaining survivors are reluctant to relive it in memory. Fortunately I found two people who were there and recalled the events as though they happened yesterday. One was Jim Sulvolis, who passed on only a few years ago; the other was 'Rose Smith', as we shall call her because she does not want her real name mentioned. She now resides at Alamosa, Colorado, on a ranch where I interviewed her in 1960. Her story follows verbatim.

★ ★ ★

"In the fall of 1913 we were living at Tioga, Colorado, in a company-owned house. The weather was bitter cold with heavy snow on the ground, when a guard rode up and said, 'You people got one hour to git out'.

"We loaded our pitiful belongings onto our old wagon, hitched our old horse, and pulled out toward Walsenburg, sixteen miles to the east. The horse had difficulty in pulling the wagon through the snow, and we had no heat in the wagon. It had a canvas top, so we rolled up in blankets while father drove. Father would stop now and then and build a fire for us to warm by and to rest the horse.

"Our family consisted of father, mother, and six children. I was the oldest, eleven at that time. We passed through many camps on the way, all deserted. All had been evicted from their company houses. We made it to Walsenburg by the grace of God and the will to live. At Walsenburg we were placed in an old building with others in our same fix, fed, and allowed to sleep in a warm room furnished by the union. But we couldn't stay here. We had to move into a camp, because there were too many coming in. So early one morning we headed for the Ludlow tent colony, thirty miles to the south. We had been given food to carry with us. Our chances of making it were slim, but we had no alternative. Walter Montgomery was at Walsenburg at that time, and when we got there he was helping take care of everybody.

"We had thought the trip from Tioga to Walsenburg was extremely difficult, but this trip was much worse. It required four days to reach Ludlow. One night we stayed in an old deserted homestead house. Another night we were taken in by a homestead family. The last day we faced a heavy snowfall and wind. Much of the time the older members of the family walked, to help the horse. It was a large tent stretched over a wooden frame of two-by-fours, and it had a plank floor. It contained a large iron cookstove for both cooking and heat, a table and four chairs. We slept on army cots.

"The monotony was terrible. We were compelled to remain inside the tent most of the time due to the severe cold. There was no school, so mother taught us from schoolbooks we had and read the Bible to us regularly. Father spent most of his time along the railroad picking up pieces of coal that had fallen from a train of coal cars. Then he would go into the foothills off about a mile and cut wood.

"I'll never forget that Christmas. Father obtained work for a few days with a rancher. Then, with this little money, he drove to Trinidad, which was to the south of us perhaps ten miles. He bought a present for every member of the family. He cut a small pine, and we decorated it with our own homemade decorations. He had killed a young deer a few days before, so we feasted on deer meat. When I look back on it now, it seems rather wonderful. Then it seemed horrible.

"Every day or so the guards would search our tent for a gun. Miners were prohibited from having a gun of any kind. If the miners had had guns the day of the massacre, the outcome would have been vastly different, but those cowardly guards fought women and children with their machine guns.

"After a long and difficult winter spring arrived in all its glory. The snow, which had remained all winter disappeared. Father would instruct us every day in what we were to do in the event of a disaster. He knew the guards were capable of anything and might decide to make war on the camp. Mother doubted this. She said, 'They wouldn't dare shoot at women and children'.

"Rumor had it that the camp was to be destroyed unless the miners returned to work. Father had taught each of the older children to take a young one by the hand and run south to a shallow canyon that ran east and west about three hundred yards south of the camp, and wait there until all arrived. The two little ones would be carried by father and mother. Hundreds of times he told us exactly what we should do.

"On the twentieth of April, 1914, everybody in the camp was outside in the bright warm sunshine. About 10:00 A.M. there was a loud explosion, such as dynamite might make. Everybody ran to their tents. Then it came. The rattle of machine guns could be heard. We waited for a few seconds. The bullets began knocking splinters from the tent frame and father yelled, 'Go to the canyon'.

"There was no mistake: they were going to destroy the camp. Every one of the children carried out their orders except me. I went into partial shock from fright and ran in the wrong direction and alone. I ran right at those firing machine guns.

"Although I was in shock that day, I can recall distinctly everything that occurred. I had gotten about two blocks when I met hundreds of women and children running in every direction, screaming hysterically. I was knocked down into a ditch, where I remained for a time. I jumped to my feet, screaming for my mother and was knocked flat again.

"The good Lord was with me that day

or I'd have been seriously injured. It is impossible to describe just what occurred. There were twelve hundred women and children in that camp. Most of the men were gone, either working for a rancher or looking for work. All of those women and children were running madly in every direction and screaming at the top of their voices.

"There was very little breeze, and smoke from the burning tents, fired by the guards, settled down over the camp. That helped the situation somewhat. Finally I managed to get to my feet. I looked wildly in every direction for my family, then just stood and screamed. The guards began shooting at me. I still have the dress that I wore that day. There are three bullet holes in it. How I kept from being killed only God knows.

"As I stood there screaming I saw Louis Tikas running toward me. He threw me into the ditch and told me to shut up, that I had just become a full-grown woman. After a while he said to me — and I'll never forget his kind words — 'We are in a bad spot, but I have been in worse. You are not a child anymore. As I said, you have grown up in the last few minutes. You must act like a grown-up if you want to live. We are going to get up from here in a few minutes, and we'll try to make it to the pumphouse. If I get hit by a bullet and go down, you keep on. Do you understand? Don't hesitate one moment, or it may cost you your life. God help us'.

"He took my hand and pulled me to my feet, and he pulled me along behind him as we ran. The machine guns were firing at us. I could see puffs of dust about us. We ran as neither of us had ever run before, and finally we made the pumphouse in one piece. We both fell to the floor completely exhausted. After a few minutes, when we had regained our breath, he called down into the well, and a kindly lady came. He told her to take care of me.

"As she started for the steps that led down into the well, he turned to me and said, 'I'm sorry I had to be so rough on you, but I had to impress upon you that you are not a child anymore'.

"The steps led down to a giant pump that pumped water to a tank above for the engines. All around the well ran a platform, called a ring-set. This caught the water that dripped from above so that it could be pumped out. The platform was about three feet in width, made so for a man to walk on. When my eyes became adjusted to the light that filtered down from above, I counted seventeen other women and children. The well was cold, and soon I was chilled to the bone.

"The only reason the firing guards did not rush the pumphouse and burn it down, as I learned later is that Louis Tikas got word to them that armed men were inside just waiting for them to come. They fired at the building all day long and we were showered with splinters. Later Mr. Tikas brought down an armload of blankets that he had taken from a locker upstairs.

"He remained in the camp all that day, aiding women and children to escape this hell.

"We remained in the well until after darkness set in. We had all but given up. We prayed often and wept. Many of the children were not with their mothers, but had been picked up by other women, and Mr. Tikas had brought them here.

"About dark Mr. Tikas came down the well and told us, 'There'll be a train in here in a few minutes. I will be between the firing guards and the pumphouse, so when I call down, come up slowly. Watch the little children, for these steps are slick'.

"We waited and prayed. Then we heard the train pull in, and Mr. Tikas called for us to come up slowly. Very slowly we walked up the slick steps, our legs hardly able to bend because our muscles were so dead from sitting in one position. As we reached the top he pointed out the canyon and said, 'Go, and wait for me, and I'll lead you out'.

"After we reached the canyon, which at this point was about five feet in depth, we hunkered down against the canyon wall and waited for Mr. Tikas. Unfortunately, he never came. We found out later that he had started for us and stopped to give aid to a lady and her children. He was captured and killed by the insane guards. Lieutenant Linderfelt struck him over the head with an army rifle, crushing his skull. Then his men shot Mr. Tikas three times in the back. A braver man never breathed a breath of life.

"After we had left the guards climbed aboard the engine and told the engineer to put that G.D. engine out of there or they'd blow out his brains. The train crew testified later to this effect — how they heard women and children run whimpering along the train side. The guards set the pumphouse afire after they discovered we were not there. Then they turned their machine guns on us in the canyon.

"We headed west, keeping well down until we were out of range. Then we moved onto the road leading west toward the mountains. We were all nearly starved, but it was much worse on the small children. They had had nothing to eat for hours and had cried themselves to sleep. We each took turns carrying them. The farther west we moved the colder it became, for we were heading into the mountains, which at that time of the year gets bitter cold at night. None of us had a coat. The ladies removed their heavy skirts to wrap the small children in, to help keep them warm. We would walk awhile, then rest. It seemed like hours, but we knew we had to get as far away from the camp as possible.

"I tried desperately not to think of my folks, but now and then I couldn't help it, and the tears would fall. I tried to hide this from the others. After all, I was only eleven years old and had always lived under the guiding hands of father and mother. But, as Mr. Tikas had said, 'You are not a child any more'.

"Later that night, as we rested, we heard shouts from men. They said, 'Don't be frightened. We are miners'. They were John and Jim Sulvolis, who had escaped the camp before the destruction commenced. They had come to the spring for water when they heard us talking.

"They took us to a log cabin, where we met their mother and brother Pete. They fed us, and John went into a herd of cattle and milked a couple of cows for the children. We rested and slept on the floor in front of a fireplace, where it was nice and warm.

"Early the next morning John rode a horse into what was left of Ludlow. When he returned he told us that the camp had been destroyed completely, that a wagon was on its way to pick us up. When the wagon came we were taken to Ludlow. All that remained was acres of burnt canvas, and bodies lying here and there in what had once been our tent colony streets.

"I was reunited with my family. None of them had been injured. A new camp had been set up near the Black Hills, just a few miles from where we had started. We moved into this camp and remained there until order was restored. There were no guards here, as all the miners were armed. Later we returned to the mines and eventually lived as humans were meant to live.

"I'll never forget Ludlow. It haunts me daily."

I next phoned Jim Sulvolis, who was living at Red Wing, Colorado, and I asked if he would relate his story for me.

He replied, "Yes, come on out, but bring a bottle. It's pretty dry out here."

I drove out to Red Wing, which was about twenty-five miles west of Walsenburg, and I did as he asked, took two bottles. I found Jim and his wife, just the two of them, living in a nice little cottage tucked away in the mountains. He was a fine man with a fine sense of humor. He said all the kids had grown up and left home, but they returned home now and then. We sat on his front porch, facing the beautiful Green Horn Mountains to the east.

He asked if I planned to have this story published, and I told him, "Yes, if that is possible. But it is so horrible that so far the publishers have passed it by."

I asked him to begin at the beginning.

"I'll take notes," I said. "But take it easy, because I can't write too fast."

After a few belts he commenced. His

many curse words I have purposely left out as unprintable. He cursed every time he mentioned the guards. Here is what he said, verbatim except for the strongest of the cuss words.

"In the fall of 1913 we were living in a company-owned house at Big Four Colorado, now extinct. I have been asked many times why we just didn't pack up and leave. We had been bucking these operators all of our lives. My answer is, we were all born and raised in one of these coal camps. We lived in a company house, ate company food, wore company clothes, drank company whiskey, and we had never been paid in cash — very little, at least. There was no place for us to go. When you have been at this business as long as we had, you become glued to it. We lived all of these years in the hope of some day living as other people live who work for a living.

"We tried homesteading near where your father lived — Walter Montgomery. Hell, man, making a living on one of these dry land farms is impossible. A man could make it only by working in the winter and dry farming in the summer.

"There were five in my family — father, mother, Pete, the oldest boy (he was twenty-five at that time), I was twenty-two, and John was eighteen. We were a religious family and attended services when possible. Not many of those hellholes had a church. None of us had ever been in trouble except with some dirty . . . guard. I mean with the real law. We hated those S.O.B's so badly that any one of us could have killed one as easily as we could a big rattler. They were inhuman bastards.

"Late in 1913 one of those . . . guards rode up to our house and ordered us to leave at once. Pete wanted to kill him, but father said, 'Pete, put that gun away'. Neither father nor mother went in for violence.

"We knew miners were not supposed to have a gun of any sort in our possession, so we hid our shotgun beneath the wagon bed. We loaded up and headed for Walsenburg. Once a guard stopped us and wanted to search the wagon. We allowed him to do this, but when he told mother to get off the wagon seat, I told him if he touched her I'd break his

281

G.D. back. I wanted to kill him. That's a terrible way to feel — I realize it now — but we had over the years built up a hatred for those . . . that knew no bounds.

"Before we reached Walsenburg we were hit by a blinding snowstorm that came directly out of the east. We pulled into an old deserted mine that had been out of operation for some time. We put Old Dynamite, our horse that had moved us hundreds of times, into a shed and fed him. We moved into the washhouse, where they had left a wood-burning stove. There was enough coal around to keep us warm for a while. We spent three days there. Then we moved out for the union headquarters at Walsenburg.

"We met and talked for some time with your father Walter Montgomery. He was a good man. I'll never forget him and his fist fights with those . . . guards. We then headed south for Ludlow. We didn't relish taking charity, but it was the only way. It didn't look right for strong, able-bodied men to sit around and do nothing.

"We finally reached Ludlow and moved

into a tent near the central part of the great camp near the west side, where we could look right into the . . . guards' camp. It is physically impossible to express our feelings for those . . .

"We hunted west of the camp, under the pretense of hunting wood. We killed jack rabbits, and twice during the winter we killed a deer. It was a horrible winter. We played cards until we almost hated each other. We shoveled snow until that made us sick. It was pure hell. Now and then father would remind us that if it weren't for the union we'd have died of starvation, that we ought to be grateful that we were still alive. We always paid attention to father although by that time we were all grown men. It was a custom, brought over from the old country, that as long as a man or boy lived under his father's roof he would obey his father's wishes. This we did mostly to humor him, but we had minds of our own that didn't agree with all Greek customs.

"When spring at last came, slowly as it always did, we began to hear rumors that the camp would be destroyed if the miners didn't return to the mines under the company's conditions. Father and mother didn't think those . . . guards would destroy a camp filled with twelve hundred women and children. We knew better. They were capable of any crime, for which they were well paid.

"When the weather started to warm up, father decided to leave and look for work with some rancher. He was compelled to sneak out at night; otherwise those . . . guards wouldn't allow him to leave. They wanted to keep track of every person, for they didn't want outside publicity.

"One day John and I slipped out of camp and headed west on a road back into the mountains. We were looking for a place to move into in the event of an emergency, which we knew would very likely come. We met a rancher whose feelings about the . . . operators and guards were pretty much the same as ours. He said he had a cabin he rented to hunters in the fall, and we were welcome to move into it for a few days or weeks free of charge. We looked it over and it was just what the doctor ordered. A large, one-room log cabin, with a fireplace and a short distance from a spring.

"When we returned we informed mother of the cabin, and she said we'd go nowhere without father. But we out voted her. Father we knew, was capable of taking care of his own affairs. In the spring, and every spring without fail, the Greeks held a celebration, whether they were farmers or not, to welcome in the crops and to thank the Lord for the beautiful spring and many more things. This celebration always commenced on the nineteenth of April and lasted until the wine gave out, which at times meant several days and nights, and all other people of the community joined in for the fun.

"Before the celebration we invited a . . . guard in for a few drinks of wine. He thought we were just being nice to him, but we were after vital information. After he became plastered, he told us it was a shame, but Lieutenant Linderfelt had orders to destroy the camp on the twentieth of April if the miners did not make some effort to return to the mines by that time.

"We made plans very carefully. We

didn't want even our neighbors to know, because a slip of the tongue might give away our well-laid plans. Quietly we loaded up our wagon with what little we had, and it wasn't much. We planned that as soon as the celebration got well under way, and when the train pulled in, with all the noise going on, we would leave. It wasn't too uncommon to see a wagon moving about after dark, hauling wood or such, and every family had a horse and wagon because they moved so often.

"So, as planned, Mother, John, and Pete got into the back of the wagon, and we slowly moved south onto the road that led back into the mountains. No one asked questions, and no one bothered us. After we had cleared the camp, Mother got onto the front spring seat with me. It was a bright moonlit night, and we could see some distance ahead. We were laughing, congratulating each other on outsmarting the . . . guards, when in front of us loomed a figure on horseback. We didn't have to be told it was a filthy guard. I told the others to keep quiet and let me do the talking.

"He stopped us and asked what the hell we were up to, and I told him we were merely going to do some work for a farmer who lived up the valley a short distance.

"He replied, 'You ain't going nowhere. You're goin' back to camp and see the lieutenant. Maybe he'll let you go.'

"I knew what this meant, but I had no choice, so I started to make the turn back. Just then a shot rang out from the back of the wagon that seemed to shake the whole valley. The guard fell from his horse. I knew Pete had shot him from the back of the wagon. Mother began screaming so loudly I thought she would alert the camp. We got her quieted down and looked over the guard. He was dead as a doornail. We held a consultation and decided we'd have to take him with us until we found a place to dispose of the body.

"I tied his feet to the rear of the wagon, and John rode his horse, and again we headed west. We knew that if we left his body behind they'd track us to the cabin. Mother never got over this killing. She prayed for us daily. But to us it was the greatest deed of our lives. We gloried in this murder. Later we realized what we'd done, and it didn't seem so great, but he'd have killed us if the tables had been turned.

A mile further on we came to a deserted homestead with an old dry well. Into the well we dumped the guard's body. We kept his rifle and revolver and what ammunition he had carried, and also his horse. We were now guilty of murder and of horse stealing.

"We moved into the cabin in good order and set up housekeeping, such as it was. It beat having to see a lousy . . . guard every time you looked outside. There was plenty of firewood and fresh water. We were almost out of food, so John and I decided we could steal food while the . . . guards were enjoying the celebration and drinking free wine. We didn't tell Mother and Pete figured it was a good idea. We needed coffee and what else we could find. So John and I set out afoot, each carrying a steel rod we had taken from an old corn planter just in case we ran into one of those thugs.

"We made the camp and slipped

around the guards' tents and located the supply tent. In front sat two . . . guards, about half drunk and singing at the top of their lungs, really celebrating with the Greeks. I told John we could just walk in like we had business there and they wouldn't notice us until we were upon them. It worked. We walked right upon them. I hit one of them with my three-foot-long rod, and John did the same to the other. Mine started to get up, and John put him out with another belt from the rod.

"We commandeered a two-wheel cart, loaded it down with groceries, and pushed it out of the camp. We had a tough time getting it over the railroad and over rocks, but we finally made the road and headed west. It was a hell of a job, pushing and pulling that cart, but it paid off. We reached the cabin safely some time in the early morning of the twentieth of April.

We were dead tired and slept until about nine the next morning. We rose, fixed our breakfast, and chopped wood until about 10 A.M. Then we heard two loud explosions, then machine gun fire.

We knew we hadn't been wrong in leaving. The . . . thugs were attacking the camp, which consisted of about twelve hundred women and children, most of the men away working or hunting work.

"We told Pete and mother we were going back. We might be able to help those people. We took the dead guard's rifle and ammunition and set out for Ludlow. From the brow of the hill west of the camp we surveyed the horrible situation. They had fired many tents, and the smoke hung to the ground like a leech.

"Those dirty bastards were making war on defenseless women and children. We fired into the camp where a machine gun was firing. We didn't have much ammunition, but we got more later. The camp was alive with women and children running in every direction. They had naturally panicked, and they ran wildly. Had they had the presence of mind to get into those deep ditches they could have crawled out of the camp. Many did later on.

"John and I entered the camp and soon ran into Tikas. He told us to throw those women and children into the ditches and tell them to crawl. He was running about like a wild man. He had more guts than any man I ever knew. He saved hundreds of lives that day by remaining in camp all day, defying the guards' fire. They wanted him, and he knew it, but he kept right on. They called him a dirty little red-leg, and he called them much worse.

"John and I kept under cover of the smoke and did as much good as possible. Once we saw a . . . guard setting fire to a tent. We waited until it blazed up good, then knocked him in the head and threw him into the fire. We took his rifle and ammunition.

"We would fire into the guards when we caught them bunched. What damage we did we'll never know, but I'll bet we sent several to their happy hunting grounds. Now and then we would have to leave the camp for fresh air. Then we'd go back. One rancher rode up near the camp to see what was going on, and he was shot from his horse and killed.

"Thirteen women and children who sought refuge in a hole in the ground were every one murdered. Before the destruction had started two little boys were wandering into the guard area. One was killed and the other terribly wounded. God only knows how many were killed that day. Many wandered into the nearby hills and died of starvation or from wounds. Tikas ran about telling women to get into the ditches and crawl, and we aided him all we could. We had to keep in the smoke. Now and then we'd hit a clear place where the smoke had lifted, but these areas we avoided. It's a wonder we weren't both killed. At the time we didn't seem to worry about this.

"We remained in the camp area all that day. When the smoke began to clear away we left. The guards were only firing a burst with a machine gun now and then. We asked Tikas about those in the well, and he said he would get them out after dark, that the guards were concentrating most of their fire on it at present, but were afraid to rush it, fearful there might be armed men inside.

We returned to our cabin. We felt

terribly ashamed that we couldn't have done more to aid those poor souls. That night after supper John and I went to the spring for water and heard the voices of women and children. We escorted them to our cabin, fed them, and the next morning they were picked up and returned to Ludlow by union workers.

"We sent John in, and he reported that the camp had been completely sacked. So we loaded up and also returned. The guards had vanished. We took the dead guard's horse with us, and the authorities told us to keep the horse until someone claimed it. We kept him until he died several years later. We never did tell anyone about the guard's body in the well.

"When we arrived in Ludlow we saw a field of blackened canvas. All that remained intact was iron bedsteads, which stuck up here and there like tombstones. We helped lift thirteen bodies from a hole where they had been murdered.

"The day of the massacre Father had been ordered to the Black Hills camp, and he missed the massacre. I accompanied him to the site the next morning, and

293

it was horrible. The exact number of women and children who were killed or who died later from injuries is impossible to determine. No names of families moving in had ever been taken. For years the massacred bodies were being found in the hills about. Early that morning eight miners and two children had been killed, and the authorities made a guess that twenty-one women had been killed too.

"The martyr of the massacre was Louis Tikas, leader of the Greek miners. On the way to help a woman and her two children he was captured by the Roughneck Company. Lieutenant Linderfelt hated Tikas, and when he found that the 'dirty little red-leg' had been delivered into his hands, he raised a Springfield rifle high over his head and brought it down on the head of Tikas. Tikas threw up his arms to ward off the blow, and both his arms were broken. Then the lieutenant brought the gun down on Tikas's head, crushing his skull. The lieutenant testified later that it was not necessarily a hard blow. Tikas staggered back a few steps and unluckily

294

turned around. Three bullets tore into his back, and he fell dead.

Linderfelt delivered the verdict, 'The damned S.O.B. tried to escape.'

"After the Ludlow massacre we moved to the Black Hills camp, and eventually back again to the mines. Many years later my conscience began to bother me about the guard my brother and I had killed and thrown into a well. I confessed the whole thing to the county attorney, who studied me for a few minutes before replying.

"Then he said, 'Jim, if you think for one minute that I am going down there to dig up those bones to make a case against you, you're crazy. Not one of those lousy bastards ever came to trial for killing those families. Too bad you didn't kill a few more of them. Go home and forget the whole thing. You have nothing to worry about'.

"Then I called on our priest and confessed to him. After some thought the priest said, 'Jim, soldiers in a war are not brought to account for the men they killed. I mean each individual. You have always been a good man, a credit to your family and to the church. You have nothing to worry about. You have been forgiven long past'.

"So I tried to forget the massacre, and I did to a certain extent. But now and then it comes back."

★ ★ ★

I interviewed a man and a woman in Walsenburg in 1960. They had been in Ludlow during the massacre. They were eight years old at that time, and their story is touching but great. They had become good friends, childhood sweethearts in fact. They were together every day, all the time, and they never missed a day of being together. The morning the sack of Ludlow commenced, he went in search of this girl. He found her took her hand, and led her out of the camp to safety. Some years later they were married, and they have a family of seven children. They were too young at that time to recall many details now, but they both remember how he led her out of camp. They are John and Emma Barker.

After the horrible massacre the President of the United States sent in troops, though too late to help those who were killed. He also sent in an investigating committee to make a complete investigation. Here is their full report:

History records no darker chapter in the long story of human exploitation than the reign of terror in the southern Colorado coal fields from 1900 to 1914.

Just how many men, women, and children met violent deaths in the unprovoked assault by armed troopers, many of them imported thugs, and professional strike breakers on the pitiful tent colony where miners and their families had taken refuge after being evicted from their company-owned homes into a bitter cold winter.

On the side of the employers was the richest family in the world, the Rockefellers, plus all the power of the subservient state, which acted as an active partisan of the owners for years in a ruthless industrial war intended to smash every vestige of organized labor in the coal regions.

Conditions that prevailed prior to the strike are described in authoritative accounts of the era as "Unbearable."

Here in brief is the situation that brought about the strike.

"In defiance of laws on the statute books, workers were refused the eight-hour day, paid in scrip, herded in company towns, compelled to trade with company stores, cheated out of from 500 to 800 pounds on every car of coal dug by them, and denied the protection of safety devices. Hundreds met death through the gross negligence of the companies, yet no damage suits were ever filed, for the operators owned the legal and political machinery, and the families of the dead were doomed to live in squalor and despair."

It was against such feudalism that the miners, after unrelenting and violent opposition to their peaceful effort to bring about a betterment of conditions, finally went out on strike. Officials of the United Mine Workers were prompt in responding to their urgent pleas for aid and gave them financial and moral support in their extremity.

Thus the U.S. Commission on Industrial Relations, appointed by President Woodrow Wilson, preceded its account of the Ludlow Massacre by describing the strike as a revolt by whole communities against the arbitrary economic and political and social domination by Colorado fuel and iron companies.

Telling of imported gun thugs taken into the so-called National Guard, the Commission said that by April 20, 1914, "The National Guard no longer offered even a pretense of fairness and impartiality, and its units in the field had degenerated into a force of professional gunmen and adventurers who were economically dependent on, and subservient to, the will of the coal operators. This army was dominated by an officer Lieutenant Linderfelt whose intense hatred for the strikers had been demonstrated."

The Commission further noted that the guardsmen were armed with machine guns and high-powered rifles and could count on speedy reinforcements, and then commented: "The Ludlow colony had been repeatedly searched for weapons during the preceding weeks, for arms and ammunition, and testimony indicates that Lieutenant Linderfelt believed the colony to be unarmed. This was the unequal lineup just prior to the 20th of April, 1914, when reports began circulating that the colony was to be destroyed."

The Commission concluded that there was ample evidence to support the charge that the Colorado National Guard was an instrument of suppression maintained for the purpose of intimidating and crushing workmen on strike in an effort to improve the conditions of life for themselves and their families.

The Montgomery family remained on the homestead until 1919, by which time most of the mines were closed permanently, worked out. All that remains of many communities are the foundations of houses, long since deserted. We sold out to a doctor and moved back from whence we had come, Springfield, Illinois.

My father, Walter Montgomery, died in December 1932, at the Old soldiers' Home in Leavenworth, Kansas. My mother died in 1941. Rube Ferns, the welter champ, died in 1944. My wife and I at present live in Leavenworth, Kansas, and every spring in June we visit the old homestead. The log house built by my father still stands intact, although it has not been lived in for many years.

In 1945 a rancher decided to deepen an old well on his place to catch surface water for his cattle. This was about one mile west of the Ludlow site. In the process he unearthed the bones of a human. These were removed and buried in an unidentified grave. With the bones were found such articles as a belt buckle with U.S. on it and bits of cloth indicating the uniform of a soldier from the World War I period. Nothing to reveal how he met his end. Jim Sulvolis said when he heard of it, "Let sleeping dogs lie."

My wife and I visit Ludlow every time

we go back to the homestead and the log house. It is extremely difficult to imagine that this peaceful place was, not so many years past, the scene of a terrible disaster. All that remains are a few empty houses — no inhabitants at all. The well where the women and children sought refuge is still in use. There is a fenced-in square lot, in the center of which is an imposing monument dedicated to the poor souls who gave their lives in freedom's cause.

On the monument there is a plaque listing the names of those who died that day. The first name is that of Louis Tikas, the Ludlow martyr for whom an unknown poet has left these lines:

Who knows what deeds of ancient
    day
gave impulse, yearnings, tendencies?
Who knows what blood flowed in
    his veins?
perhaps the blood of Pericles.

He braved the assailant's iron might,
their brutal hate, unbridled, wild,
his trust the miner's naked home,
his care the mother and the child.

And men in stress of coming days
shall win strength his spirit gives
who so for justice yielded life,
He, dying, yet immortal lives.

Oh, Louis Tikas, gallant soul,
defender of the helpless, weak,
knight of humanity, you were
more than American or Greek.

Heroic spirits of all time
attest your manhood's strong avail,
extend warm handclasp as the cry,
Good brother, noble comrade, hail!

That in substance is the story of
Ludlow — not the whole story, which
can never be fully told. There are too
many missing parts.

A Drunk's Redemption

This story was obtained from Manley Justice's daughter, who lived for some time in Leavenworth, Kansas, and from other members of the family. His granddaughter said, "I've heard the story so many times that I can recall every detail. It is embedded in my memory, never to be erased."

MANLEY JUSTICE came from a well-to-do family of religious farmers. When about fifteen years of age he became addicted to alcohol, although none of his family ever touched alcohol in any form.

He had been born near Springfield, Illinois, in 1846, and, according to members of the family, he was the black sheep. They kept reminding him of this until it got the better of him and caused him to want to be free of them. He hated farm life, and when he was sixteen years old he ran off from home to seek his fortune elsewhere. By that age he was already a giant of a man, about five feet ten inches in height and a hundred eighty pounds in weight.

After leaving home his first job was that of cleanup boy in a Springfield saloon. He had drunk whiskey before, but now he had it readily at his disposal. He soon became a drunken sot. He remained in this city for about a year and was ordered to leave town when he was suspected of stealing.

He met the same fate in St. Louis, where he hired out as a teamster of a freight wagon train heading west. At Kansas City he was fired and again ordered out of town. He then went to Topeka and later on to Fort Riley, where he obtained work and was jailed for stealing whiskey. He was hired by a freight-wagon captain, who told the commanding officer that he could handle Manley. He didn't know Manley.

About three days out of Fort Riley Manley stole the captain's whiskey and headed out over the vast prairie, soon to become drunk and lie down to sleep.

When he awoke, the train had vanished. He started walking and was soon captured by a band of roving Osage Indians who took him to their village, beat him, and hung him by his feet from a tree. All night long the squaws poked him with sharp sticks and the children threw stones at him. A man of lesser stamina would have succumbed, but Manley was not an ordinary man.

The next morning a young buck cut him loose, and he fell to the ground. The buck tied his feet to a horse and rode out across the prairie, dragging Manley behind, over rocks and brush. All at once the buck cut Manley loose and rushed back to the village. Manley sat up in the long grass and saw a band of Indians riding toward the village, evidently enemies of those who had tortured him all night.

Manley made his way to a creek, drank his fill, then headed west, walking in the creek, expecting to be captured again at any time. That night he slept in the brush and the next morning continued walking west. In the distance he saw a detachment of cavalry and made his way to them. They took him back to their camp. Here he was treated by the surgeon and put to bed to recover.

The kindly doctor unwisely gave Manley a drink of whiskey. In those days whiskey was quite commonly used medicinally. Of course, it only fired Manley's insane desire for drink. He watched until the doctor left his tent, then stealthily crept in, broke open a chest, and stole a quart of devil's rum. With it in hand, he left the soldiers' camp and disappeared across the plains. He wandered about until the bottle was empty, then lay down near a stream in a stupor. While he slept he was discovered by another band of hostiles. They happened to be Cheyennes. They mounted him on a horse and took him to their village, which was under the leadership of the great Roman Nose, whose correct name was Saltz Bat.

He was unceremoniously dumped in the street in front of the chief, who sat smoking a corncob pipe and rocking back and forth in a rocking chair that had been picked up along the Santa Fe Trail, where it had evidently been cast out by people to lighten their wagon load. At

307

the start of a journey people would pile everything they had on a wagon. When the team began to suffer from the grind of pulling the wagon day after day across the plains, a piece of furniture would be dumped here and there along the way. These items were usually picked up by local homesteaders or anyone who found them. Often such furniture could be seen piled around a trading post for sale.

Roman Nose was the only chief of the old Western Indians ever known to show compassion for a white man or fellow Indian. He admired courage and despised a coward. He never intentionally allowed his braves to kill women or children. Yet he gave the soldiers trouble along the great buffalo range of the Smoky Hill River which he always claimed belong to his people, and he never signed a treaty. Many times he would place Fort Wallace under siege for days at a time, allowing no one to leave or to enter and he frightened homesteaders off the range.

Once his braves brought to him a twelve-year-old white boy who had wandered too far from a train. Roman

Nose kept this boy for a year during which time the boy taught him to speak English after a fashion. He spoke it in a guttural monotone that was barely comprehensible, but he understood it. After the year he returned the boy safely to an army post. (The boy didn't want to leave, incidentally, but had no choice. The chief had named him "Boy with No Horse." This boy's story was published years ago in many magazines.)

Manley got the surprise of his life when he looked up and saw the chief in a rocking chair and he was further surprised when the chief spoke to him in English. He asked Manley what he was doing on the great plains with no horse or gun.

Manley told him the truth, that he had stolen whiskey from the pony soldiers and had wandered out onto the plains and was picked up by Indians. Once before, he told the chief, he had been captured by Indians, who beat him terribly. He showed the bruises that covered him from head to toe.

The chief seriously doubted his story and figured he was wanted by the soldiers for a far more serious charge than stealing whiskey. He decided to hold him. Perhaps the soldiers would pay ransom in cows for his return. The chief called a young Indian girl and instructed her to treat Manley's wounds.

When she came, Manley was struck by her beauty. Her skin was light, her hair was black and curly. She was about fifteen years old or a little older and slight of build. He had never seen her like since coming West, and he hadn't seen much of anything else either. She escorted him to a nearby creek, where she bathed his many cuts and bruises with an ill-smelling salve made from animal fat. She then returned him to the chief.

The chief told him, "You'll have the run of the camp, but if you attempt to leave, you will be killed. You are being held for ransom."

The chief told the girl that Manley was her ward, that she would remain with him during his stay, and that he would be bound at night. He knew that Manley would escape if he could. Manley didn't know it then, but a great change was in store for him. He was admired by this girl as well as by the chief. They showed him the first respect he had ever known, and he realized for the first time that he was a human being, a thing he had usually been made to doubt by his family's attitude to him.

The chief told Manley that the girl was a slave who had been captured in a raid on an Osage village. She was half white, her father having been a white trader and her mother was a Cheyenne. The chief said that he would have married her except that he was aware his other wives would have killed her the first time they had a chance. They hated this girl. If it had not been for his strict orders that they were not to harm her they would have killed her already.

Every night Manley was bound hand and foot. Although the girl remained by his side, she refused to release him, for she knew what the chief would do to her if she should allow him to escape. Her name was Red Flower.

After a week had passed Manley realized he was in love with this girl. He tried to make her understand, but she did not know a word of English, and he not a word of Indian. But the feeling was mutual. For her too, this was the first human to treat her with kindness. No Indian male ever showed a woman any compassion; he just brought in the food for the woman to cook while she raised the children. Whenever a woman became ill, other women attended her the husband never coming near.

One morning as Manley and Red Flower emerged from their tent, or tepee, a young buck confronted Manley, yelling and jumping up and down. This drew attention from all the others in the camp. The chief informed Manley that this brave accused Manley of taking his woman and wanted to fight him for the girl. Unbeknown to the girl and Manley, the chief had purposely set up this fight, for he wanted to test Manley's courage. He wanted him to take this girl to his own people. She was half white and did not belong in an Indian village. But he would not give her to a coward.

Manley had never in his life put up a fight, but he was well aware that he had to fight now or die. There was no way out. The young buck threw his knife into the ground in front of Manley to indicate that he would tear him apart with his bare hands.

The buck grabbed Manley and racked his arm over Manley's half-healed sores. This caused Manley to cry out and sent him into action he would normally have been incapable of. He threw the buck against a wagon wheel, which stopped him in his tracks. Then he grabbed the buck and threw him bodily into the wagon. The buck saw he was losing face, so he grabbed his knife from the ground. When he did, the chief handed Manley a spoke from a buggy wheel — all was fair in love and war.

The buck cut at Manley with the knife, and Manley knocked him to the ground with the spoke. He tried to rise, and Manley struck him again. This time the buck did not rise. The chief handed Manley the buck's knife and indicated that he should kill the fallen Indian. Manley threw the knife to the ground. This pleased Roman Nose.

Unfortunately, Roman Nose had made a deal with the soldiers for which he was now sorry. They expected him to turn over Manley to them in exchange for two milk cows. Now the soldiers appeared on the scene to claim Manley.

When Red Flower discovered that she could not accompany him, she became hysterical, threw herself on the ground, pulled her hair and screamed at the top of her lungs. Manley tried to tell her that he would return and claim her, but although she guessed at what he was trying to tell her she could not believe that he could manage. She was convinced that 'the long knives' would kill him as they always did Indians. Roman Nose soothed her by telling her that he would take Manley from the soldiers even if he had to raid their camp. So be it!

The soldiers took him and departed. The chief called one of his warriors, whom he knew to be friendly with army Indian scouts, and instructed him to find out where Manley would be held, and to do it quickly before the soldiers could take him to the fort for trial. He was sure that Manley had committed some crime for which the army would make him pay.

It turned out that Manley was being

held in a tent, and a soldier sat beside him, armed with a club and instructions to crack Manley over the head should he cause any problem. He was in no position to give much trouble, for he was bound hand and foot. They failed to anticipate the cunning of Chief Roman Nose.

That night, when all was still in the field camp of the pony soldiers, Manley's guard heard a strange noise outside the tent. He stepped out to investigate. There was a dull thud. Then in stepped Red Flower. She cut Manley loose and bade him follow her. They crawled out of the camp and departed at a slow trot. Manley could not stand much of this because of his poor physical condition after all he had suffered. They were compelled to resort to a fast walk. She could have kept up the fast pace all night long, but Manley was a weak white man. She vowed silently that she would make him as strong as Roman Nose.

At daylight she led him to a hilltop covered with rocks and heavy bush, where they remained all of that day. She went out and killed a young buff calf with her knife, built a smokeless fire, and they ate by hand.

She dried some of the buff meat by the fire to take along and eat in the daytime when they would not be able to build a fire. She could have eaten the meat raw, but for Manley it had to be cooked. He marveled at the ability of this young girl. He didn't realize it then, but she had lived by her wits all her life. She had the agility of a mountain cat and the prowess too. He felt they would never make it to Western civilization, as it was at least five hundred miles to Denver and the only weapon they had was the long sharp knife she carried.

Roman Nose had instructed her to follow the setting sun, toward where the hills were covered with snow. Here they would be safe, and free.

Next morning at daybreak they climbed down from their hilltop and were met by the brave with whom Manley had fought. He brandished his knife at Manley, for he hadn't given up on this girl yet. He would no doubt have killed the unarmed Manley, except for the swift action of Red Flower. She threw her knife deep into the back of the young warrior then took his scalp as he died. This sickened Manley. It was bad enough to kill a man, but to take his scalp he couldn't stand. Her motto was that of all Indians, survival of the fittest: kill your enemy and take his hair to prove the kill. It was no more than a way of life for her.

They moved out, keeping near the river for protection. On the plains they could be seen for miles by the enemy, both Indians and the 'long knives'.

After days and days their clothing was worn out, and they became almost naked. Both were barefoot. Red Flower was accustomed to that, but Manley was not. His feet cracked open from the sand of the desert, and he could hardly walk. At night she helped him soak his feet in the cool waters of Smoky Hill River. One day they found part of a discarded tablecloth. This she quickly fashioned into a makeshift dress. After a while Manley became hardened by his continuous walking and the diet of buff meat.

Many days after they had escaped the soldiers' camp, long before Manley could see the spot in the distance, Red Flower made the sign that a white man on horseback was coming their way. She wanted to hide and kill the rider. Manley had other ideas, of which she showed her disapproval by screaming at him. He wanted to talk to this man, to find out where they were and how far from civilization. He had spent so many days seeing nothing but plains that at times he doubted if they would ever get to a resting place.

When the hunter saw they were unarmed, he brought up his rifle. Manley held up his hand for peace, and the man lowered his rifle. He began asking questions Manley evaded as well as he could.

The man said, "I've seen everything on the plains, but this beats all — a large white man and a young Indian girl, both practically naked and with no gun or weapon of any sort."

He was clearly dumbfounded.

Finally he asked Manley, "What'll you take for the squaw?"

Manley answered, "She isn't for sale. She's my wife."

The man said, "I reckon I can take her if I'd a mind to," and he pointed his gun at Manley.

Red Flower had already smelled trouble, and she had moved out of the man's line of vision. When she saw him raise his gun, like a striking snake she threw her knife deep into his back. He fell from his horse, badly wounded.

He begged Manley, "Please don't kill me!" For he had dropped his gun and was now helpless.

Manley had to contain Red Flower; she wanted to finish the man off immediately. He took the man's muzzle-loading rifle and ammunition and helped him back onto his horse and sent him away.

Red Flower screamed and yelled at Manley, making it clear that she thought he had turned loose their enemy. She attributed such action to the weakness of a white man. She was fully aware that if the man reached camp, he would send out others to avenge him. She kept watching the back trail, and after some time she saw what she had been expecting — a man riding slowly as he traced them.

She grabbed Manley's arm and pointed out their hunter. Again she wanted to wait in ambush, for she understood that this man was bent on killing them. This time she had her way. Manley had begun to appreciate her cunning. She made him backtrack some distance, then walk back in the same track and step into the brush. Many great trackers had been fooled by this trick.

They waited silently, and the man came on. When he had passed their hiding place, Manley stood up and challenged him. The man turned with a pistol in his hand, and Manley shot him. Red Flower ran in, and before Manley could restrain her she had scalped the stranger. Then she went into a war dance. When Manley searched the man for money, he found a couple of gold pieces. He stripped the man of his clothing, gave Red Flower his shirt and kept the pants for himself. The shoes were too small to be of use.

Manley dragged the victim into the brush. His rifle was of a better make and condition than the one he had, so he left his and took the better one. He had killed his first man.

When they set out again, Manley noticed that Red Flower was wearing the man's scalp at her side. He said nothing to her. In time he would have to teach her the ways of the white man. At present they were to her worse than the Indian ways. The only thing that betokened her half-white heritage was her skin, which was very light for an Indian. She had lived her entire life among the Indians and had no memory at all of her white father's people.

As they plodded slowly across the plains they came to an island in the Smoky Hill River. Manley's feet were in bad shape, and they decided to remain here and rest for a few days. The island was covered with thick brush and rocks, an ideal place to hide. They bathed in the river and washed their clothing, and rested in the shade while Manley soaked his feet. The one thing that almost drove him to distraction was the lice he had contracted from Red Flower and the others in the village. The water rid him of the live ones, but the eggs remained and hatched.

Every day Manley tried to teach Red

Flower a couple of words of English. She proved an apt pupil. Manley soon realized that half the Indian language was composed of signs, and he learned some of them quickly, but not the dialect. She would speak a few words of English, accompanied by signs, and that way they succeeded in communicating. Manley was extremely kind and gentle with her and spoke softly. About this time he started calling her Mary, after his mother.

One day she grabbed his arm and made the sign that two Indians were approaching on horses. To do this she held up two fingers and made a galloping motion with her fingers, then the motion of shooting an arrow. This all indicated two men (Indians) on horseback. Manley now realized that one reason the Indians used the sign language was that it was silent. They could thus communicate without uttering a sound, whereas if they spoke out loud they could be heard by the keen ears of an enemy.

The two Indians had evidently become aware of the presence of these two on the island. Red Flower knowing that white women were weaker than Indian women, exposed herself enough to lead them to believe that she was a white woman. This caused them to become careless. They dismounted and came crawling up to the island under her watchful eye. She motioned Manley to shoot one, that she would take care of the other. This time Manley obeyed. He shot one through the head. The other jumped up to dive into the river and got Red Flower's knife in his back. Again Red Flower scalped the two corpses, but this time she washed them according to Manley's instructions.

Manley had now reached full maturity. He was as strong as Roman Nose and as tough as a buff bull. He could walk or trot for hours without tiring. Red Flower had made him into a different person, and this he slowly began to realize.

They saw many trains in the distance and saw many men on horseback, but they shunned them all. They thought the soldiers were probably looking for Manley.

Had they known the true situation — that the soldiers in this part of Kansas had never heard of Manley — they might have acted differently.

Red Flower said years later that these were the happiest months of her life. Up to then they had few problems and were as free as birds. She tried desperately to get Manley to remain on the prairie and continue to live as they had been living all this time. But of course Manley wanted more than this. He wanted a family with children — and civilization.

One day as they walked toward the setting sun they saw a lone wagon halted on the prairie. Closer observation revealed that it had a broken wheel and was occupied by a man, a woman, and three children. Manley indicated for Red Flower to remain in hiding while he talked to those people, as perhaps he could give them a hand. It was against her will, but she obeyed the man she loved.

When Manley approached, the man took up a shotgun, for, obviously, he and his family had never seen the likes of this stranger with long hair and beard and almost naked. Manley spoke to them politely and said he meant them no harm.

"Perhaps I can be of help," he volunteered.

They had an extra wheel, but no way to raise the wagon so that it could be put in place. The wagon was then unloaded except for supplies they had bought at a nearby trading post. Manley took hold of the back end of the wagon and the box came up. He then crawled under the axle and with his powerful back raised the whole wagon. He held it while the man put on the new wheel.

The people were very pleased and offered Manley anything they had that he could use. He thanked them and said all he wanted was salt. They gave him a small bag of that, so he bade them farewell, ignoring their questions. He was aware that they watched him while he joined Red Flower and disappeared with her over the great rolling hills.

A few days later an Indian rode down on them from a hilltop before they could hide. As he neared, Manley took a quick shot at him that only wounded him. He turned and rode off. Manley and Red Flower both knew that he would be back with friends. Manley had fired too quickly for a good shot. Again they had to go into hiding. "They found a likely spot along the river and waited. He loaded his rifle and checked it. He had only one shot.

Finally Red Flower saw two bucks following their tracks and told Manley. They waited, prepared for a fight. The two bucks rode in not too close and waved a white flag on a stick. They wanted to talk, it seemed, but Red Flower knew that they really intended to come in under a flag of truce and then jump Manley when they were close enough.

They were much surprised when Red Flower told them in the Osage dialect that there would be no powwow, that they had better leave. They had taken her for a white woman. They argued, but agreed to nothing. Finally, one of them pulled up a bow and fired, out of range. They were deadly accurate at close range, but at a distance the bow was useless. Manley had his rifle laid over a tree limb, and when the buck had fired, Manley also fired and one of them fell dead. The other rode off.

Manley thought they were now in a worse fix than before because his last shot was gone. Yet for some unknown reason the Indians did not come back. Later Red Flower and Manley were followed for some distance, but at last they lost the hunters.

One day they saw an old deserted house in the distance, and after they had made certain that no one was about, they approached the house and found two apple trees loaded with green apples. When they were off about fifty yards, a shot rang out and Red Flower fell to the ground. She had been shot through the calf of the leg.

Manley immediately picked her up in his arms and ran toward the river. They were in the open with nothing to use as protection. Otherwise, Manley might have first found out who had fired at them. It definitely was not an Indian.

He washed her wound and tied a piece of cloth around it, after placing mold on it according to her directions.

They had to leave. They couldn't remain here too long, for whoever had fired at them might follow. He took her on his back as he would a child, and they headed out over a great hill. In this manner they could see anyone who might be following, and they could also see the winding river.

The next morning, when they had not progressed very far, Manley saw a wagon train circled near the river. He made for the train. Red Flower screamed at him not to go near the wagons, for these people were enemies. Nevertheless he went. He wanted something for her wound, and these people had it. When he drew near he was met by three men armed with rifles. They told him to come in, but to leave the Indian girl outside — a scout had recognized her as Indian, and they were afraid.

Manley placed her on the ground and went into the circle. The train's people gaped at him as though he were a prehistoric monster. A barefoot giant of a man, with long beard and hair, his clothing in shreds. Yet he talked intelligently. He told them that the girl had been shot and that he needed white cloth and anything they could spare to treat the wound. The train's captain was very courteous. He gave Manley salt, white cloth, a bottle of ointment for the wound, and a bottle of whiskey. One woman, when she found he was not bent on killing them, gave him a dress for Red Flower. The captain also gave him a burro that had been following the train and a half-grown pup.

As he thanked them and started to leave, an elderly lady gave him a quilt and said, "Take care of her. She is one of God's children."

Manley set Red Flower on the burro, which had been broken to ride by the children of the train, and he pulled the pup with a rope. At the river he removed the dressing from the wound, poured whiskey on it, and gave her a drink of this fiery stuff. Then he wrapped the wound in the clean white cloth. He did not touch the bottle of whiskey because he had vowed never to take another drink, and he kept this vow for the rest of his life. He placed her near a fire and cooked her a buff steak in the coals. Never had she dreamed of being treated in this way by a man.

They stayed by the river for three days.

When they left, she was riding the burro, followed by the shaggy pup, which she had named Great Bear after an Indian chief. Manley led the way. He had been informed by the train captain that they were about fifty miles from Fort Wallace. It was clear by now that the soldiers were not looking for Manley, so he moved onto the road. When they met a train or a person riding, they moved off to the side in order not to be seen.

When they were nearing Fort Wallace they saw a detachment of soldiers coming their way, and Manley decided to talk with them. Red Flower wanted to run for the brush. All her life she had been taught that these were enemies, but lately she had been letting this white man whom she had accepted have his own way, so she remained quietly seated on the burro.

When the detachment saw the two of them, their commanding officer halted his command, and a scout rode out to meet them with the lieutenant. Manley greeted them warmly and asked if they had a surgeon with them. The officer said they had, and Manley asked if the surgeon could look at Red Flower's wound. The surgeon dressed the wound and told them it was healing nicely — no infection.

They talked for some time, and Manley told them of how he and Red Flower had walked all the way from Fort Riley.

The lieutenant said, "That's the most incredible thing I ever heard of."

They moved off the road, and, as the troop passed them, the flag was dipped and the soldiers raised their hats.

When they reached Fort Wallace, or Pond Creek as it was called prior to being named Fort Wallace, they stopped in front of the trading post. Manley left Red Flower who by now was getting used to the name Mary. She remained out in front while he went in to make some purchases with the gold he had taken from the man he killed.

He purchased a shawl, a dress, a mirror which she had never seen before, beads, a comb, and other things she had never owned. He bought for himself a pair of pants, a hat, and a shirt. Above all he purchased salve for killing lice.

As he emerged from the store he saw

a big two-hundred-pound buff hunter trying to engage Mary in conversation. He was speaking in her dialect, but she turned her back on him and refused to answer.

Manley dropped his purchases and struck the man in the face with his fist, knocking him flat on his back. He lay there, looking up at Manley.

Then he said, "I'm the man who shot her in the leg. I ain't going to shoot you in the leg. I'm goin' t' put a ball between your G.D. eyes."

He started to draw his pistol only to find himself looking into the barrel of Manley's rifle. He dropped the pistol.

"I ain't through yet, Mister," he grumbled.

Manley replied, "If you ever cross my path again, I'll kill you on sight. I would have killed you right here, but there are others here that I'd have to fight at the same time."

Manley gathered his belongings and headed for the river where he and Mary made camp and had a celebration, bathing and getting rid of the infernal lice. Then they dressed in their new finery. She was so fascinated with the mirror that he finally had to take it from her.

That night, as they slept near the fire, a shot was fired at them. The only thing, perhaps, that saved them from being killed was that Mary had washed out their old clothing and hung it to dry on a bush near the fire. Whoever had shot at them must have mistaken these clothes for themselves.

Manley grabbed his rifle and stealthily crawled around the rocks behind where Mary and he had been sleeping. She followed with her knife in hand. Soon they saw the figure of a man approaching the fire. He evidently thought he had shot Manley, and he had no fear of her because Indian women were not taught to shoot guns. He had underestimated this wisp of a girl.

Manley shot the man through the body, and he fell, mortally wounded. Mary ran in and took his scalp before he was dead. She finished him off with her knife. It was the man Manley had struck outside the store. They searched him and found about $100 in gold.

Manley tied a rope to his legs and dragged him to the river and shoved him in.

They immediately broke camp and headed west, keeping away from the road, fearful that the man's body might be found before they had put enough distance between them. They had about a hundred and seventy-five miles more to travel, and the nights began to get cool. They could not waste time and so moved along as rapidly as possible. About fifty miles further west they again took to the road.

One morning a herd of cattle came into view, driven by two men who were having trouble getting along. Manley talked to them, and they offered him a job helping them drive the herd to Denver. He accepted. He had already cut his hair and beard and therefore presented a much better appearance than he had at any time since leaving Riley.

Although there were millions of buffalo still on the plains, cattle were much in demand in the gold fields and usually brought a fortune in gold. The cattle drover told Manley of a sawmill west of

Denver where he could probably obtain work.

"It's next to impossible to hire men there," he said, "because all the men want is to pan gold."

Red Flower had her greatest surprise of all when they reached Denver. She saw Indians camping on the outskirts of this great village, which at that time had a population of about 5,000. She saw Indians walking up and down the streets, and actually saw white children playing with Indian children.

Manley went out to the sawmill and was immediately hired, for it was not often that such a man applied for work. They gave him a house to live in, all furnished. Here Red Flower, under her new name of Mary, had her greatest problem — adjusting to the ways of a white person, living in a house and sleeping in a bed.

She and Manley were married that year in December. The next spring they loaded up and moved to the gold fields. Like the others, Manley was bitten by the gold bug.

After three years in the gold fields

Mary told her husband she wanted to go back to the plains. They homesteaded fifteen miles east of Denver and became successful in cattle raising. Of their union six children were born, and a number of their offspring still live in the Denver area.

Mary wanted to see her mother if she still lived. Through an Indian agency Manley located her living at the Mayetta Reservation near Topeka. They rode the train to Topeka and found her mother who at first did not believe that this was her daughter. But Mary refreshed her memory of things that no other woman could have known.

They then visited Manley's family near Springfield. This was a great reunion, for his relatives had thought he must be dead all these years.

In 1890 the doctor told Manley that he ought to take his wife back to the mountains because she had a lung ailment. The high altitude might help her condition. She died in 1896 and was buried on the ranch where they had lived for so long. Without her Manley was a lost soul. He began worrying about the men he had killed, and he found it impossible to go on without his wife.

One day he was found dead in bed, a pistol by his side. He had taken his own life. He was buried next to Mary on the ranch, not far from where they had walked and helped drive a herd of cattle to Denver many years past.

Postscript: These writers visited the ranch, and the house built by Manley had been burned to the ground. A new house stands in its place, owned by his grandson. The graves are marked by beautiful stones surrounded by an iron fence and well kept.

Kate Bender — Devil's Disciple

WHEN the Reverend John C. Cole, Sr., one of the most respected ministers in the state of Missouri, died in 1950, among his effects his son found a written confession claiming to be that of 'Kate Bender'. It was written in longhand, supposed to have been taken down at the dictation of this woman with the expectation that it would be made public at her death. However, when she did die in December 1935, Cole refrained from making the confession known, perhaps partly because he was not certain that it was authentic and partly because he could see no purpose in divulging it.

Permission was granted us by Rev. Cole's son to read the document and copy it for publication. Cole had attached the following letter to the confession:

To Whom It Might Concern:

Although I am of Protestant faith, it is not uncommon for an elderly member of my congregation to call at my residence and ask me to hear a confession. They usually have some little thing preying on their mind, and this gives them a greater feeling of security.

When Dorothy Hamm called, as we have known her for years, I was not in the least surprised, thinking she wanted to discuss some church function. In this respect, she was very active. Then she informed me that she was the notorious Kate Bender. I could not believe it. But when she began her confession, all doubt left my mind.

No human on God's green earth would confess to this diabolic existence, unless she was that person. She spoke of murdering innocent people with no compassion or compunction, as though it was a common everyday occurrence. I knew it could be none other than Kate Bender. The promise I made her to have it made public I did not keep. I decided she should be judged in the

hereafter, rather than the present.
(signed) Reverend John C. Cole, Sr.

The confession follows verbatim:

I was born December 13, 1850, in Chicago, Illinois, and christened Mary Ann Barree. My father was a harness maker and considered well-to-do by the standards of that time. Both parents were deeply religious.

By the time I was ten years old, it was whispered that I was possessed of the devil, that I was a witch. I can truthfully say that I never in my life practiced witchcraft in any form, although I was gifted with the ability to speak with the departed.

I had not the least respect for other people's property. I loved to hurt people. I would intentionally destroy small children's playthings, just to hear them weep. I took great delight in killing small animals. I surpassed all in my studies and accepted this as a natural consequence. I lived in a world filled with people I hated.

One time, the first time, I had the

urge to kill, my father switched me. When I didn't cry out, he struck me with the back of his hand, causing my lips to bleed freely. I still did not make a sound, but I did tell him, looking him directly in the eyes, that should he ever lay a hand on me again I would kill him. He knew I meant it and never touched me again; he was afraid of me, which pleased me considerably.

At the age of fifteen I cursed a boy severely, and he threw a stone at me. This infuriated me to the extent that I enticed him into the basement of a deserted house and killed him. I buried him with rubble. It was some time before his body was discovered; I was not surprised.

When I reached the age of seventeen, I was considered a beautiful, mature woman. One day I decided to visit my grandfather, who lived alone on a farm. I was forbidden to go there, but I went because I hated to be directed like a child. He embraced me as he would a harlot, and I struck him with my hand several times.

He took a switch and switched me

until I had large welts on my backside and legs.

He said, "I'll teach you something, you mean little slut?"

Then he ordered me to return home. I stood and watched him chop wood. I playfully picked up the small ax, and, when he bent down, I struck him until he expired. I walked calmly to the shed, obtained a spade, dug his grave and shoved him in, covering him with twigs and brush. I surveyed my work with pleasure and returned home.

A week later I overheard my father say, "Grandpa is missing. A search party is being organized, which I will join?"

I was fearful of being detected, so I stole money from my father, walked to the station, and purchased a fare to Kansas City, Missouri.

I found Kansas City a dirty place, but as active as a beehive. This meant money, and I had to find employment. I encountered no difficulty and was soon working at a desk as assistant to the head bookkeeper of a wholesale grocery firm who supplied traders from the West. This gave me a chance to observe the men who came from the West, and the large amounts of cash they carried on their person impressed me. There was no credit for them: it was cash.

I wanted to be rich, I wanted to rule, and I did to a certain extent. I mulled over in my mind a foolproof plan by which I could relieve some of the men of their money and not be detected. I would need an accomplice, so I picked out a boy who worked for the firm. He was big and strong and not too intelligent. His name was John Hardwick. After hearing my plan for riches and realizing he could earn more in one robbery than he could earn with the firm in a whole year, he readily agreed. I informed him in no uncertain terms that, should he ever speak one word of our plan to anyone, I would kill him.

After finding a secluded spot near the river I enticed a fine young man from the West to take me buggy riding. When we reached the spot and the young man had his mind on improper advances, John Hardwick struck him with a large hammer. He produced about $300, of which I gave John $50 with the promise of more later. We placed the body in the buggy and shoved it into the river. The horse we released to roam as he pleased.

Being gifted with the ability to speak with the departed, I rented a furnished house on the outskirts of town and began holding seances. Actually I was looking for a likely prospect among them.

One day I read that an elderly lady wanted to hire a handyman. I told John I got this from the spirit world, that this lady had money hidden away, but I was guessing. John and me called on her, and she hired him immediately. She lived in an old mansion and alone.

Over the ensuing weeks I became very friendly with her, posing as John's sister. One day she directed him to go to the village for some items, and he watched her as she went to her hiding place for the money. He informed me of this, so we set our plan with perfection.

As she and I sat in the yard talking, John struck her with his heavy hammer. We placed her body in the well and covered it with trash and rubble. We then searched the house and found almost $700 in money. We set fire to the old house. As it was some distance from any other residence, it was some time before it was discovered. By the time neighbors arrived the house was almost consumed with flames.

I was aware that John would likely be questioned, so I composed for him a likely tale, which they accepted without doubt. They deducted that she had been caught by the flames and burned.

One day Alfred and Myrtal Holtz came to me and asked to speak with a departed relative. I saw in these two just what I needed to perfect a plan I had in mind. They were German, having been in this country but a short time, and the departed relative instructed them to do my bidding and they would be handsomely rewarded. They were both large and strong, and they readily agreed to my plan to make them rich.

I planned to move onto the prairie along a well-traveled road. Here I could rob men heading for the far-off places, dispose of their bodies, and none would be the wiser. I had talked to traders and knew just what I wanted. I would need a fine team and wagon, so I began looking for a prospect.

An elderly man came to the firm for a load of supplies for a trading post in the West, so I enticed him to our home for a night of fun. And he came, but he did not fetch his team and wagon. Rather, he came on horseback.

We buried him in the backyard in a grave prepared for him. I gave John his horse, then prepared a note for him to pick up the team and wagon. The team was of magnificent large blacks, and the wagon was of the large type. We loaded up what furniture we would need, set fire to the house, and left for the West. I loved fires, loved to see the flames, and I set many when I was at home as a child.

When we reached Topeka, Kansas, I turned immediately south and continued until we reached a desolate spot between Thayer and Cherryvale and not far from Independence, Kansas. The place was just what I planned for.

The nearest neighbor was three miles off, and a busy highway ran nearby.

We purchased lumber and built a house. It was 24 feet square with no partitions. Beneath the floor we dug a cellar, or dungeon, with a trapdoor in the floor, in which we could drop our victims until burial time. Alfred built a rock barn and set out many fruit trees. From all outward appearances we were but honest homesteaders. No one called or bothered us while we built, they were too busy with their own affairs to be concerned with another dryland farmer family.

Our first victim motivated me into the grocery business. He came with a large load of staple groceries and stopped to water and feed his horses and to rest himself. We buried him in the newly plowed ground in the orchard and set up a grocery store, placing a sign along the road for all to see: GROCERIES AND LODGING. I sent John off with his team and wagon to sell. I also advertised with handbills my ability to cure all ailments and of my ability to converse with the outer world. I made no charge for the seance. I only wanted to judge the neighbors.

It was fall now, with not many on the road, but a few did stop, one a salesman from Topeka. He soon professed his undying love for me. I was a beautiful woman, and this was understandable.

His name was Henry Faith. I informed him that I was very fond of him but that I did not want a free boarder, and he must display his worth in money before I would consider a wedding. He displayed about $500, and we buried him next to the old man with the groceries.

During this first winter I returned to St. Louis and lived like a queen while the others tended the farm. There were no killings during the winter of 1871, but in the spring things picked up considerably, especially after I returned. Mr. Brown came, a real nice man. We sat and talked for some time before Alfred struck him. His purse was well packed. We had placed a canvas across the room so the striker could get close to the victim without being seen. We'd sit the victim near the canvas.

There were several we did not bury in the orchard. John took them out on the prairie and buried them and sold their teams and wagons. Mr. McKinney came, and we buried him in the orchard with the others. Then Mr. McGroaty we also buried in the orchard. The names of many I disremember.

Several we planned to strike escaped. One, a priest, came to spy on us. He asked questions which were none of his business, so I told John to strike him. He saw John come with the hammer and said, "I must see to my horse, a storm is coming up." He mounted and rode off. Then another man escaped almost under the same circumstances.

A crazy old woman, who carried a shotgun, came several times, so we decided to scare her off and we did.

She never returned for her gun. There was a fine lady whom I allowed to leave. She came for a saddle I had borrowed. I liked the saddle and wanted to keep it, so I told John to strike her. But he refused. Twice I ordered him, and he refused. She discovered what was going on and ran down the road screaming. We let her go, and I kept the saddle. Had she waited, I would have returned it.

The beginning of our downfall was Mr. Longcores and his daughter, who was five years old. We struck him, and I wanted to take the little girl off and leave her where she'd be found, but the others talked me out of it. We placed them in the old well.

The end of our affair came with Doctor York. He was from Independence. Dr. York and I sat and talked for some time, and I, knowing full well I should not harm him because he lived too nearby, had him struck. Had he not displayed the large amount of money he carried he would have gone free. We buried him in the orchard with the others.

There was another young man named John Rose. He came and sat in the right spot, but just as John swung the hammer he moved and was struck on the arm. He ran out and escaped on foot over the prairie. John chased him for a spell but failed to overtake him. Rose reported this to Colonel York who was in search of his missing brother, so he came to our house. He demanded to know what had happened to his brother, as he was last seen near our house, and there were many others who were never seen again after visiting us. He cursed me, called me a slut and other names when I informed him that I knew nothing about his brother. But I advised him to return alone the next day and I would hold a special seance and find his brother.

He sarcastically yelled, "I'll come back tomorrow and have the authorities with me, and we'll search this hellhole."

With this he rode off.

I ordered John and Alfred to hitch the team. We were leaving. I gathered what personal effects I desired to take with me. We headed through Topeka and on north, John and I riding on the seat, with Myrtal and Alfred in the back. I doubted, and I was right, that any one would suspect a beautiful young lady and her brother of being the Benders. We were never questioned by anyone.

Some time after leaving Topeka we turned east and crossed the Missouri River into Missouri. Later we crossed the Mississippi River into Illinois, where I decided that the others had served their usefulness. I purchased poison and placed it in the food we were to eat. John became suspicious and rode off to a small town after I gave him money. I knew he would return drunk, as he had become addicted to strong drink. Alfred and Myrtal expired that night after supper. I waited for John, and he helped me push the bodies into the river. Then I began to work on John. Knowing men as I did, I knew what he'd do.

He responded perfectly to my plan for him. I sweet-talked him into an embrace, then stabbed him with a short knife I had prepared for him. I did not attempt to bury him but left him lie as he fell. He cursed me to his last breath.

When I reached St. Louis I sold out and moved into a hotel. I could well afford it. Later, when I became restless, I accepted a position in the grocery store of George Hamm. We were later married. He died in 1910 of natural causes. I moved the store and operated it until 1923, when I sold out and moved to Springfield, Missouri, where I have lived since.

In the not too distant future I will meet my maker and pay for my sins, but before you pass judgment remember: I was born without a soul, and my hand was guided by the devil.

The name Kate Bender has no significance. I assumed this name from the boarding house where I lived in Kansas City, from Bender's saloon across the street.

I have made this confession to the best of my ability. My memory does

not serve me as well as it once did.
(signed) Mary Ann Barree,
also known as
Kate Bender and
Dorothy Hamm.

The Family That Went West

The following was related to me by one of the most fantastic men of the Old West, bar none. Pat Wagner of Western Publications gave me permission to rewrite it after it appeared in *Frontier Times*.
— W.M.

IN 1925, on a ranch near Fairplay, Colorado, I knew a man named Lige Redstone who could neither read nor write. Yet he became a very successful cattleman and was highly respected by all who met him. I'll never forget his words of advice when he hired me: "I'm givin' you a good horse and saddle. Take care of this animal like he was your own. If you ever strike him, you're fired, no questions asked."

One time I was trying desperately to handle a young colt. He jerked loose and kicked at me, and I fell into a water trough. Lige laughed heartily from his perch nearby.

Finally he said, "Montgomery, in order to teach a colt anything, you gotta be smarter'n the colt."

This story he related to me a little at a time. When he had nothing else to do and the weather was bad, he'd invite me into his great rock-and-log mansion, and in front of a giant fireplace blazing with huge logs he would rear back in an easy chair and talk as I made notes. The words that follow were his own, expressed in the idiom of Arkansas he spoke as nearly as possible as I can reproduce it.

I'd been away to the war for two years, and that's where I heard of the homestead land in the West. They told us the President had fixed it so's poor folks like us could get land free, just for farming it and building a house and barn.

I don't know where Pa and Ma was raised, but the rest of us was raised on sixty acres of the poorest land in Arkansaw, near Russellville. I was twenty years old then, George was seventeen, and the twin girls, Clara and Sara, was fourteen. Ma and Pa was nigh onto forty. We just lived from hand to mouth, never had anything, never had enough to eat, nothing to wear.

Pa and Ma would just sit and do nothing. They claimed they was born to be poor and there weren't nothin' they could do about it. I told Pa about the free land, and he said, "It takes a heap o' money, and we ain't got none." Ma sided with him. When I tried to talk about leavin' this terrible place, he'd look off into the brush and say, "Reckon I'd better get old Joe and tend the still."

I asked Ma if Pa ever sold any of that stuff he made, and she said, "No. Everybody's got a still o' their own. They just drink it."

I kept tellin' him that the stuff he made was poison, but he'd pay me no mind, just kept drinkin' it. One day I heard of a gatherin' at Honey Grove School, so I went, didn't have nothin' else to do. The preacher was tellin' these people about the free land. Everybody talked about it, that's all they done, just talk.

I remember the preacher's words. They

fired me. He said, "The gover'ment ain't goin' to bring this land to you folks. You got to get off your behinds and go after it, work hard. Most of you think all you have to do is pray and the Lord'll give you what you want. Let me tell you, the Lord ain't goin' to hand you nothin', and I can promise you that. If you work hard and prove you're in need, the Lord'll help you if you got it comin. On the other hand, if you want to sit and starve, He'll help you starve."

After the gatherin' was over I went to the preacher and asked him where this land was and how to get to it.

He looked off into the brush for a long time, and then he said, "Lige, you got more'n most o' these folks — I don't mean more money. I know you ain't got none of that. I mean more on the inside and the outside too. I believe in my heart you really want to go. People ain't goin' to help you because you're poor, and people always look down on poor folks. If you want to go, don't let nothin' stand in your way, and when it gets real bad and there's no other way, call on the Lord, and he'll likely give you a hand. Good luck and God bless you. You're goin' to need it, and remember it's up to you. It'll be a fight every step o' the way."

I went home with a heavy heart, for I knowed what Pa and Ma would say when I told them what the preacher said. Then I got down on my knees and asked the Good Lord to give me a little help — I wouldn't need much, just enough to get Pa off his behind.

The day it come we was all sittin' on the porch out of the hot sun, nobody talkin', just sittin. We heard a horse and buggy comin' the creek way. We never had no company, and we wondered who could be out on a day as hot as this'n.

Ma 'lowed, "It's probably somebody lost, more'n likely?'

When he come in sight, it was old man Brassfield, who owned all these hills and the land. He just rode up, got down, handed his lines to George, and said, "Tie up my horse.'

George didn't like the old man because he was rich, so he said, "If'n you want 'im tied, tie 'im y'self?"

Pa yelled at George, "Tie up that

horse, or I'll take a pole to you."

We all knowed Mr. Brassfield had come for money, and Pa'd put him off as usual. He just sat down. The sweat was pourin' off him like he'd just come out of the rain. He always wore a long coat, made no difference how hot it was.

Ma said, "He wears it 'cause it's the style — all rich folks wear 'em."

Pa asked Mr. Brassfield if he'd like a drink, and he answered, "Yes, right out o' the creek, none o' that filthy stuff you make."

Then he commenced, and I knowed right off my prayers'd been answered.

"Lige," he said, "I got some discomfortin' news for you."

Pa told him, "We never git no other kind, so go on."

He told Pa we'd have to move. He'd sold all this land. We had a week to get out, or he'd get the sheriff.

Pa jumped up and grabbed a pole and woulda hit that old man if I hadn't took it from him.

Pa yelled and screamed and asked Mr. Brassfield, "Where the hell kin we go?

Ain't no place fer us 'cept right here."

Mr. Brassfield got into his buggy and drove off, leavin' Pa and Ma about to go mad. Ma 'lowed we couldn't leave on account of her folks bein' buried on the place.

I called George and the twins over to me and told 'em what I had in mind. They hated this place as bad as I did and wanted to get away. Pa could fix up the old wagon, sell the cows and hogs, which wouldn't bring much. Ma could do the packin'. Pa asked where we was goin'.

I said, "Colorado, God's country. We'll get a free homestead."

Pa wanted to know what we'd use for money. I told him that George and me would cut wood for Old Man Summers. We'd get a dollar a day and work till we was ready to pull out.

The onliest thing Pa took for himself was several jugs of mule whiskey and just the clothes he had on. About the first of May 1866 we set out with one loaded-down wagon and a team of worn-out horses. It was slow goin', an' all the folks along the road told us we'd best turn back, that the Indians'd kill us sure, we orta leave one behind to tell the story. I knew it'd take more'n talk to turn me back. I wanted to be free of this godforsaken country.

About four days later, all the rims on the wagon come off. So George and me had to push the wheels to the river and let 'em soak up tight.

About a week later one old horse just laid down and died in the road. Right off Pa said we'd put George on the other horse and send him back to Ma's folks on the White River and git us a horse so's we could go back.

I told Pa, "If you want to go back, go on, but the rest of us is goin' to go on."

I told Pa and Ma to push and the rest of us would pull with the horse. Pa cussed for thirty minutes, but we moved the wagon.

I said, "If we have to we'll push it all the way, but we's goin on, no difference what."

Later a man we didn't know rode up and set on his horse, lookin' us over. He asked what in tarnation was goin' on. I told him the whole story, that we only had thirty dollars and was stuck sure. He asked if I was aimin' to push that loaded wagon all the way out West.

I said, "We will if we have to. We ain't goin' back."

He said, "A man that is willin' to push a wagon five hundred miles needs help, so I'm givin' you a horse. When you git where you're goin' and git on yer feet, I want fifteen dollars."

We hitched the horse and got ready to pull out, but first I got down on my knees and thanked the Lord for his help.

Ma said, "Lookit Lige down there waller'n' in that dirt like a hog, gone clean out o' his mind."

I told her I was only thankin' the Lord fer his help.

She said, "The Lord didn't have nothin' to do with it. It was that feller back there."

"But the Lord made him do it," I insisted.

She wasn't very much on religion then. Before the trip was over, though, she was a firm believer in the Lord.

It took over a week to git to Fort Smith, and the preacher was right — people made fun of us, and none offered to help. We didn't want no help. We wanted work so we c'd pay our way. George and me found work for a few days, but nobody'd let us go West with them. We was just too poor. We headed for Coffeeville [sic], Kansas. It was out of the way, but we didn't know it. We made it fine for a few days, then some Indians took after us. They was friendly-like at first. They wanted whiskey, guns, and everything else we didn't have, 'cept Pa, and he refused to part with any of his mule whiskey. He said it was again' the law to give Indians whiskey, and I told him 'twere again' the law to make it, too. They finally rode off a piece and fired some arrers at us but didn't hit nothin? I told Pa he should let me shoot one.

He said, "Not unless they jump on us."

One evening some wagons pulled around us and made camp, so for protection we pulled in close and camped. The head man of this outfit come over and told us to move. He didn't want no white trash close to him, said we'd steal somethin' an' he'd have to shoot one of us. Him and Pa got to yellin' at each other. This man made a run at Pa, an' I tripped him. He fell headlong on his face in the dirt.

He jumped to his feet, and him and me clinched. I was strong as a bull an' Pa always said, "just about as smart." I weighed about two hundred, and this man was about the same size. I'd learned a lot about fightin' in the war, and he didn't scare me none. We fought all over the place, with all his folks lookin' on. I finally got him in his hair and throwed him again' a wagon wheel. He dropped cold, like he'd been hit between the eyes with a boot jack.

I was plum' glad as I was nigh spent. Then I looked up, and here come another man at me. He looked like a buffalo bull, lightin' mad. He had a knife in his hand, and I yelled for Pa, who didn't have to be called — he was there.

Pa yelled at this man, "Hold on there, right where yer at, er I'll put a minnie ball twixt yer eyes."

The man held fast. He knowed these mountain men could shoot the eye out of a squirrel off a hundred yards. He just told us to move on, that they didn't want us nigh them.

Pa had his dander up and he was plum' hot, so he said, "If there's any movin' to be done, you'll do it. Git out o' here, and now."

The man moved on back to his wagons. The next day we follered them to Coffeeville. They was slower'n us 'cause they was drivin' bulls.

We couldn't find no work in Coffeeville, so we lit out fer Independence, Kansas. It was just like Coffeeville, so we set out fer Wichita, Kansas. We knowed it was a long piece, so we bought more beans. I hate beans to this day. A couple of days out I killed a young bull calf, and, believe me, we et like we'd never et before, plum' starved for fresh meat.

We had too much — it'd spoil. So Ma dried some for the trip. A few days after Independence, as we was eatin' supper, in rode three men, trail-weary. They asked for a bite to eat, an' we fed 'em. We had it made up between us that if anybody rode in, one of us was to go around the wagon and take up his rifle.

One asked after he'd et, "Got any

money? If you say No, we're goin' to look y' over, so you'd better have somethin'?"

I was lookin' at 'em down the barrel of a .45 – .70 when they looked up and I said, "You men git out o' here and be quick?"

They mounted, and as they rode off, one turned and fired his pistol into the fire. I shot 'im plum' outa his saddle. We mighta been white trash, but couldn't no man outshoot one of us. I got to 'im first and put his poke in my pocket. I been sorry for this all my life, stealin' from a dead man. I knowed the Lord wouldn't like it. We drug him off the road so's he wouldn't be seen.

Pa said, "Lige, you hadn't orta done that. They'll have the high sheriff down on us, sure as yer alive."

I told Pa, "It'll be a few days before he's found. It's a long way from any town."

The next afternoon two men commenced firin' at us from some distance. We sneaked behind a little ridge and looked them over an' figured them to be the two who paid us a visit yesterday.

Pa said, "I might be able to hit one from here."

I handed him my .45 – .70. He laid down on his belly and aimed a long time, and when he fired we seen one feller jump and fall. He'd been hit hard.

I done the same thing again, got there first and took his poke before George and Pa got there. Later, when we camped, I went into the brush and counted my stolen money. I had six twenty-dollar gold pieces. This was a lively town, people everywhere talkin' about gold in the West. We didn't want to get rich overnight. We just wanted some work. We found it and stayed a week, then set out fer Great Bend, as it was later called. I'll bet we crossed the Arkansaw River a dozen times. We went through another place, maybe Hutchinson, I don't rightly know.

Many asked us if there was anybody else out there on the prairie. We met some comin' and some goin', not many, but we kept on, even after bein' warned by soldiers of the hostile Indians. We thought when we got to Wichita we were almost in Colorado. When they told us we'd just got started, it made me feel bad, but I was goin' on, I didn't care how far it was, even a thousand miles. Anything was better 'n what we'd left. While in Wichita I bought two repeating Winchesters and two .45 revolvers and plenty of ammunition. I knowed by asking others that it was goin' to be worse 'n hell and we'd need these guns. Pa and Ma wanted to know where I got the money, and I wouldn't tell them. They guessed right. Pa said he'd never fire one of those guns cause they was tainted with stolen money.

One day we asked some travelers for directions, and they headed us for Fort Larned. When we reached this fort, it was the first time since we had left Arkansaw that anybody'd treated us right. Here they treated us great. When they seen we was goin' on anyway, they gave us powder and shot fer the muzzleloaders, water barrels, and one old scout drawed us a map, and told us to keep headin' into the settin' sun and we couldn't go wrong. The girls could read this writin' — the rest of us couldn't. Before we left, a army colonel came and talked to us.

He said it took a brave family to do what we'd already done, but from here on it'd get a lot worse.

He said, "You'll find many small bands of Indians looking for small outfits like yours. They'll figure you are just plain farm folks and can't fight. When they come at you, kill a few, and they'll let you alone until another band strikes. I know you men can shoot. That'll be in your favor."

He went on, "Keep your eyes peeled. Don't let 'em surprise you. One man walk in front and one in back, and when they come, put the women and girls on the floor of the wagon and pray to God the Indians don't get them."

He gave us a compass and told the girls how to understand it to keep us going west. We made it fine for about a week. Then we run into a big band of Indians. We seen 'em way off and was ready when they got to us. We unhitched the team and took off the harness, and George held the horses so them crazy Indians wouldn't scare them to death.

We had two heavy boards to get behind, and when they come in close, yellin' and carryin' on, me and Pa each got one. Pa was shootin' the Henry, and I was tryin' the new rifle for the first time. They rode off. They didn't expect what we gave 'em.

Pa said, "Lige, you take the .45 – .70, and when they come again, get the one that's painted up like the devil himself."

They couldn't shoot, but I never seen such ridin' in my life. The one I was lookin' fer rode in close. All I could see was his foot. I shot his horse, and when he went down he throwed that Indian thirty feet. When he got to his feet I downed the Indian with the Winchester for good. Pa got another one too. So they rode off.

Then I seen our horses tearin' across the plains, the Indians chasin' 'em. They took our horses, and here we was again with no team.

Pa said, "If you hadn't stole that money, this'd never happened."

Pa grabbed his jug and took a long pull of it. I told him he orta leave that stuff alone, it'd kill him sure if he kept at it. He said he only drunk it to get the dust outa his throat.

Them devils just set off some distance and talked. They didn't like our brand o' shootin'. Then I seen them ride off behind a little hill and build a fire outa buff chips. The ground was covered with 'em. They had some jugs they'd got somewhere, and they begun drinkin.' Soon they was yellin' an' carryin' on like they was havin' a real fine celebration. It musta been as bad as Pa's stuff. They'd take a drink, jump up and down, beat theirselves on the chest, and yell.

I seen two of 'em ridin' off and figured they was goin' fer help. Later those two came back with more jugs. George and me took turns watchin' 'em. They all got drunk, screamed and yelled, but they never come back after us — why, I don't know. Figured they'd do it later, when the whiskey'd be gone, I reckon. Or figured they'd get us when we set out on foot.

They yelled an' bellered 'way late at night, then they all laid down and went to sleep. I told George we'd wait a spell, then go get our horses while they was asleep.

He said, "Lige, you're crazy. I ain't hankerin' to get ketched by them Indians."

I told him, "I ain't hankerin' to walk and die of thirst, with nothin' to eat, either."

But he give in, and when we figured the time was ripe, we moved in, makin' sure no guard was around. We crawled in on all fours. At first the horses made a little fuss, but they settled down as we cut them loose, all of them. We got out with ours and rode them back to our wagon. Every Indian horse we'd cut loose follered us back to our wagon. We hitched and moved out, follered by about twenty-five horses. We picked two good ones and tied them to the wagon. The others one at a time drifted off. We often wondered what them Indians thought when they woke up and found their horses gone.

We went for a long time, maybe six days, and didn't see any Indians. Then I was walkin' back of the wagon and George was in front when six Indians slipped almost upon us. I started to shoot and seen one wavin' a white rag tied to a stick. I knowed from the war that he wanted to talk. So I motioned him to come in.

He rode in and dismounted. He said he wanted us to give him the girls — they had seen them and Ma walking — so he could trade them to the soldiers, then we'd get them back. He talked pretty good English. We found out later that he'd been sent to a school and was so ornery that they kicked him out.

As I listened to him, I leaned my rifle again' the wagon. I had a idea. So I grabbed this young buck and throwed him to the ground. I told Ma to fetch me a rope. I tied his hands behind him, then jerked him to his feet, and put a knife to his throat. His eyes bugged out like he'd seen a haunt.

I said to him, "You tell them varmints back there if they give us any problem, I'm goin' t' cut your head off."

He did what I said. Then I tied him to my belt so he couldn't run off. We went down the dusty road with him walkin' like he enjoyed it, and his friends backed off a hundred yards.

After a long time I seen them Indians tearin' out across the prairie like the devil was after them. Soon soldiers showed up, about fifteen of them with three wagons.

I told the sergeant what had happened, and he said, "I'll just kill this boy."

But I talked him out of it, for the time anyways. That night we made camp along the road. The soldiers camped with us. They tied the young buck to the wagon wheel, and when they all got to sleep I cut the boy loose. He mounted and rode off.

The sergeant was mad when he found out what I'd done, and he said, "He'll come back and cut off yer head. You people never learn."

That Indian was a fine-lookin' young man, and I knowed the sergeant was goin' t' kill 'im, and he hadn't done us no harm.

The soldiers took us to a tradin' post, as they called it. It was nothin' but a hole in the ground with logs over the top and covered with dirt. We stayed there four days after the soldiers left, to rest up our horses and ourselves. I forgot to mention the buffaloes on the plains. There was millions of 'em everywhere. Sometimes we had to shove them outa the way, and there wasn't no shortage of meat.

The day we got ready to leave the post, about twenty Indians rode in, surrounded us, and took all our horses, every one. They didn't take anything else, and I figured the trader had been in on the deal. Here we was again, with no team, and God only knew where.

I got down on my knees — I remember it well — and I said, as I looked up into the sky, "Lord, it's me again. Looks like all I ever do is ask fer help, but this time it's fer Ma and the girls too. Pa, George, and me can take care of ourselves. Bringin' Ma and the girls was my fault, not theirs. I'd like to get them to some town where there ain't no Indians. So if it ain't askin' too much, I'd like fer you to give 'em a hand, and I promise not to bother you again."

We talked to the trader. We didn't have no money to buy a team with.

He studied fer a spell, then asked, "C'n you men build a house? If you c'n, when it's finished I'll give you a team and see that you git to Denver or

Pueblo, whichever you want."

There was nothin' to do but take 'im up. He gave us a tent to live in and gave us some food — it wasn't much, but better'n beans and buff meat, which we had all got tired of.

We worked day and night, all of us, even Ma and the girls helped. One day while we worked I looked up and there set an Indian, the buck I'd cut loose. He grinned, and I seen he wanted to be friendly, so I quit work and went over to him.

He said, "You one time do me great favor, now I do you good. No more Indians bother you!" And he rode off.

The man at the trading post — I think it was called Howe's Station — he said about the boy that he was now a chief because his Pa'd got killed. He was an Osage.

About the middle of October we was ready to move out. We'd decided on Pueblo. It didn't make much difference, we didn't know one place from the other. The man gave us a team and wagon — our'n was plum' spent — and we headed out once again.

When we got to Pueblo, winter had set in and it was snowing. We got a job cuttin' railroad ties. The man was real glad when he found out we wasn't huntin' gold. He gave us enough lumber to build a big one-room house. For the first time in our lives we had food, clothes, and a fine place to sleep.

We had our first real Christmas in Pueblo, and it was a great day. When the spring come in 1867 we was ready to look fer a homestead. All of us worked all winter and saved all we could, which was more'n any of us had ever dreamed of. So, after gittin' some facts about the country, we lit out fer Fairplay about one hundred miles west.

First George homesteaded 160 acres about 45 miles south of Fairplay. I went on south till I found the place I wanted, and it's this place right here, er part of it. I added on a lot since that time.

Several years later, George and me went back to Arkansaw. Ma's only regret at leavin' that place was leavin' her folks buried there, because they never had no regular burial by a preacher. When we got back here with their remains, we had a regular funeral, like they'd just died. They were buried along the road back there with Pa and Ma. Ma was eighty-six when she went, and Pa went a year later.

While we was back in Arkansaw we found the man who'd give us the horse when our'n give out and died. We found the old man livin' with his daughter. We told him we'd come back to pay for the horse. He didn't have no idea what we were talkin' about, said he hadn't sold no horse, in fact he hadn't had no animals fer years. But after we told him, he remembered. We had a long talk, and he said he wished he'd a gone with us. We paid him fifty dollars for the horse — he only asked $15, but we figured the interest and all, he deserved it.

I had one more debt to try and square. I'd put this off fer a long time, so I went to our preacher and told him.

"Lige," he said, "you've done a lot of good in your time, and I reckon if the Lord wanted to punish you he'd a done it long before now. I figure on the great Judgment Day you'll find you got a clean slate."

The two men we killed back on the prairie we found out was wanted by the law for killing a family, and the other 'n, when they caught him, they figured he'd killed his two friends, so they just hung him.

Postscript: I left the Redstone ranch in 1926 and joined the army. In 1940, when I visited the ranch with my wife, Lige was still going strong. We had a great visit, and I returned in 1965 to visit his grave. The little graveyard is near the road going into the ranch house. His gravestone is a large flat stone about a foot thick. Inscribed on it is, 'Lige Redstone, born 1846, died 1944. He will always be remembered'. On the stone is a statue of a pure white horse. — W.M.

Other titles in the
Ulverscroft Large Print Series:

TO FIGHT THE WILD
Rod Ansell and Rachel Percy

Lost in uncharted Australian bush, Rod Ansell survived by hunting and trapping wild animals, improvising shelter and using all the bushman's skills he knew.

COROMANDEL
Pat Barr

India in the 1830s is a hot, uncomfortable place, where the East India Company still rules. Amelia and her new husband find themselves caught up in the animosities which seethe between the old order and the new.

THE SMALL PARTY
Lillian Beckwith

A frightening journey to safety begins for Ruth and her small party as their island is caught up in the dangers of armed insurrection.

CLOUD OVER MALVERTON
Nancy Buckingham

Dulcie soon realises that something is seriously wrong at Malverton, and when violence strikes she is horrified to find herself under suspicion of murder.

AFTER THOUGHTS
Max Bygraves

The Cockney entertainer tells stories of his East End childhood, of his RAF days, and his post-war showbusiness successes and friendships with fellow comedians.

MOONLIGHT AND MARCH ROSES
D. Y. Cameron

Lynn's search to trace a missing girl takes her to Spain, where she meets Clive Hendon. While untangling the situation, she untangles her emotions and decides on her own future.

NURSE ALICE IN LOVE
Theresa Charles

Accepting the post of nurse to little Fernie Sherrod, Alice Everton could not guess at the romance, suspense and danger which lay ahead at the Sherrod's isolated estate.

POIROT INVESTIGATES
Agatha Christie

Two things bind these eleven stories together — the brilliance and uncanny skill of the diminutive Belgian detective, and the stupidity of his Watson-like partner, Captain Hastings.

LET LOOSE THE TIGERS
Josephine Cox

Queenie promised to find the long-lost son of the frail, elderly murderess, Hannah Jason. But her enquiries threatened to unlock the cage where crucial secrets had long been held captive.

THE TWILIGHT MAN
Frank Gruber

Jim Rand lives alone in the California desert awaiting death. Into his hermit existence comes a teenage girl who blows both his past and his brief future wide open.

DOG IN THE DARK
Gerald Hammond

Jim Cunningham breeds and trains gun dogs, and his antagonism towards the devotees of show spaniels earns him many enemies. So when one of them is found murdered, the police are on his doorstep within hours.

THE RED KNIGHT
Geoffrey Moxon

When he finds himself a pawn on the chessboard of international espionage with his family in constant danger, Guy Trent becomes embroiled in moves and countermoves which may mean life or death for Western scientists.

THE WILDERNESS WALK
Sheila Bishop

Stifling unpleasant memories of a misbegotten romance in Cleave with Lord Francis Aubrey, Lavinia goes on holiday there with her sister. The two women are thrust into a romantic intrigue involving none other than Lord Francis.

THE RELUCTANT GUEST
Rosalind Brett

Ann Calvert went to spend a month on a South African farm with Theo Borland and his sister. They both proved to be different from her first idea of them, and there was Storr Peterson — the most disturbing man she had ever met.

ONE ENCHANTED SUMMER
Anne Tedlock Brooks

A tale of mystery and romance and a girl who found both during one enchanted summer.

TIGER TIGER
Frank Ryan

A young man involved in drugs is found murdered. This is the first event which will draw Detective Inspector Sandy Woodings into a whirlpool of murder and deceit.

CAROLINE MINUSCULE
Andrew Taylor

Caroline Minuscule, a medieval script, is the first clue to the whereabouts of a cache of diamonds. The search becomes a deadly kind of fairy story in which several murders have an other-worldly quality.

LONG CHAIN OF DEATH
Sarah Wolf

During the Second World War four American teenagers from the same town join the Army together. Forty-two years later, the son of one of the soldiers realises that someone is systematically wiping out the families of the four men.